THE IRENAEUS TESTIMONY TO THE FOURTH GOSPEL

The Irenaeus Testimony to the Fourth Gospel

Its Extent, Meaning, and Value

By
FRANK GRANT LEWIS

WIPF & STOCK · Eugene, Oregon

Wipf and Stock Publishers
199 W 8th Ave, Suite 3
Eugene, OR 97401

The Irenaeus Testimony to the Fourth Gospel - Its Extent, Meaning and Value
By Lewis, Frank Grant
ISBN 13: 978-1-60608-279-9
Publication date 10/17/2008
Previously published by University of Chicago Press, 1908

PREFACE

The reader will observe the narrow limits of the following discussion. It makes no claims to grappling with "the Johannine Problem," nor with the general problem of the fourth gospel alone, nor even with the single question of the authorship of the fourth gospel. I have simply set myself the task of discovering what the testimony of Irenaeus to the fourth gospel is and of estimating its significance. My essay, therefore, deals with only one aspect of the problems mentioned above. That it is an important aspect, however, will not be denied. Even when the study of Irenaeus leads to an elimination of his testimony from the factors which have to do with the Johannine question, as the study of Harnack did, the study is recognized as essential and significant.

That the question of the significance of the Irenaeus testimony is a mooted one cannot be evaded. When Ernest F. Scott, one of the latest and most suggestive writers on the fourth gospel, in the preface of *The Fourth Gospel: Its Purpose and Theology*, says: "It may be granted that the external evidence is not sufficient to warrant a decisive verdict on either side," the situation appears to be hopeless. He was undoubtedly influenced by the immense difference in the conclusions of Lightfoot, Harnack, Bacon, and Zahn, in view of which it might seem that nothing more can be said. The very diversity of their conclusions, however, raises the question whether some more common and more tenable ground may not be discovered. This is to be done, nevertheless, not by a mere combination of these important views, but by a fresh examination of all the data involved. Such an examination I have endeavored to make.

The crucial question is: Did Irenaeus have actual knowledge of Christian affairs in Asia at the close of the first century? If this essay makes any contribution toward answering this question, it is through a more careful criticism and evaluation of the Irenaeus testimony attributed to Polycarp and the presbyters, as it bears upon that question, than has been made heretofore.

In view of the present condition of the text of Irenaeus, nothing more practical appeared possible than to use the Stieren text without criticism. This could be done with the less hesitation because, as the discussion endeavors to show, the meaning and value of the Irenaeus testimony to the fourth gospel must be found in a more general interpretation than that which bases its conclusions on mere variation of text. No theory can be secure which hinges on uncertain, or conjectural, readings. Fortunately there appears opportunity for a theory in which such readings may largely be disregarded.

I have freely laid under tribute all available works which offered assistance. This puts me under obligation to many for whose suggestions only this general acknowledgment can be made. I am grateful to all. I am particularly indebted to Professor Ernest DeWitt Burton and to the researches of a seminar conducted by him in The University of Chicago during the autumn of 1906, in which the entire field of the external evidence to the authorship of the fourth gospel was patiently examined. If I have here succeeded in going beyond that study and finding what, until now, has been overlooked in Irenaeus, this is largely due to the suggestive criticisms of Professor Burton which were received in that seminar and others which he has given in the preparation of this dissertation itself. I need hardly add that it has been a personal pleasure to have my independent study work out in accord with his "booklet" theory of the composition of the gospel.

FRANK GRANT LEWIS

NOVEMBER, 1907

CONTENTS

CHAPTER I

	PAGE
THE EXTENT OF THE IRENAEUS TESTIMONY TO THE FOURTH GOSPEL	9

Table showing extent from point of view of the gospel.—Inferences from this table.—Table showing extent from point of view of the progress of Irenaeus' work.—Inferences from this.—Conclusion

CHAPTER II

THE AUTHOR OF THE FOURTH GOSPEL FOR IRENAEUS	17

The gospel the work of John of late apostolic times.—Irenaeus knew only one John, other than John the Baptist and John Mark, of apostolic times.—The writer of the gospel an apostle.—Irenaeus' usage of the word "apostle."—The writer of the gospel the son of Zebedee

CHAPTER III

THE VALUE OF THE IRENAEUS TESTIMONY FOR US	24

Irenaeus not critical.—Irenaeus' relation to Polycarp.—Trustworthiness of the letter to Victor.—Trustworthiness of the letter to Florinus.—*Heresies* 3.3.4.—The meaning of the Polycarp testimony concerning the John of Asia.—Concerning the Johannine writings in the time of Polycarp.—Application of this conclusion to *Heresies* 3.1.1c and to 3.11.1a. —Irenaeus' relation to the presbyters and other unnamed men.—Conclusions of Lightfoot, Harnack, and Zahn.—Further investigation of the data.—The presbyter material was oral

CONCLUSION	57
APPENDIX: RESULTING HYPOTHESIS FOR THE JOHANNINE QUESTIONS	61
INDEX OF NAMES AND SUBJECTS	63
INDEX OF IRENAEUS REFERENCES	64
INDEX OF NEW TESTAMENT TEXTS	64

CHAPTER I

THE EXTENT OF THE IRENAEUS TESTIMONY TO THE FOURTH GOSPEL

The extent of the Irenaeus testimony to the fourth gospel is in itself significant. What that extent is may be seen from the following tables.

The first table is an arrangement of the references to the testimony from the point of view of the gospel. It serves especially to show how much of the gospel Irenaeus used, what parts were of particular interest to him, and, indirectly, the portions which he did not use.

The second table is an arrangement of the same references from the point of view of Irenaeus' work. It calls attention particularly to his attitude toward the gospel as that attitude is to be seen at different stages of the progress of his discussion.

The tables are intended to present the references and, at the same time, to offer some interpretation of the testimony to which the references direct. In order to make such interpretation, certain abbreviations and symbols are employed. These are of three classes:

1. Those which precede the references to the gospel. Here—
No symbol = an exact quotation.
  v = a quotation varying merely *verbally* from the Westcott and Hort text, and so not materially affecting the sense.
  s = a quotation varying from the WH text in *sense* as well as verbally.
  r = any looser *reference*, not a quotation.

By an "exact" quotation is meant, where the Greek is preserved, an agreement with the WH text; where we have only the Latin, a Latin reading which seems to represent the WH text. In some instances indicated as "exact" quotation, however, only a part of the verse, or verses, of the gospel as referred to is quoted; but the quotation is "exact" as far as it is used, even when, as in some passages, words of interpretation are fused with the quotations (e. g., 4.25.3b).[1]

It may be added that Irenaeus often used language which is colored by the influence of the gospel but which does not show a sufficient number of the words of the gospel to warrant calling it even a "reference." His language received such coloring from the thought of the prologue especially. But the prologue was the part of the gospel which he liked particularly to quote. In view of this, there is less occasion to attempt to include among the references every passage which indicates even a coloring from the gospel.

Still further, it is to be noted that these tables do not include such passages

---

[1] All references are to the *Adversus Haereses*, unless otherwise indicated.

in Irenaeus as mention the name of John but mention it without making a quotation from the gospel or a reference to it (e. g., 1. 9. 1*b*).

2. The abbreviations between the references to the gospel and those to Irenaeus, showing the authorities to which Irenaeus attributed the portions of the gospel indicated by the references preceding them. Here—

Ap = Apostle　　　　　　　　JA = John (apostle, as shown by context)
C = Christ　　　　　　　　　　JD = John the disciple of the Lord
DL = Disciple of the Lord　　　L = Lord
G = Gospel　　　　　　　　　　S = Son of God
GJ = Gospel according to John　Sc = Scripture
J = John　　　　　　　　　　　W = Word of God, or Word

References not accompanied by any of these abbreviations indicate passages of the gospel which are either introduced without any external authority or those which are introduced with an authority of such indefinite kind as to make it of no considerable value.

The John indicated by the abbreviation JA is not to be understood as distinguished from the John indicated by the J alone. Frequently the passage combines the two in such manner as to leave no doubt that the two are one. The separate indication of those passages of the gospel which are, by the context, attributed to an apostle is merely for the convenience of reference in study. It is to be understood, also, that these are not the only passages which, as the context shows, are to be attributed to an apostle (cf. pp. 18–20).

3. The abbreviations following the references to Irenaeus. Here—

a advises the reader that the passage of the gospel indicated in the first column will be found somewhere within the first third of the section of Irenaeus indicated in the second column.

b refers similarly to the second third of a section.

c refers similarly to the last third of a section.

This division and notation has been found convenient in the preparation of the essay. Perhaps it will be equally convenient for any reader who may wish to examine the merits of the discussion for himself.

TABLE I

Showing Irenaeus' use of the fourth gospel from the point of view of the gospel. The numbers in the first column refer to the chapter and verse of the gospel; those in the second, to the *Adversus Haereses*, except one passage preserved only by another writer, which is referred to as "Fr. 35," according to the numbering of Stieren.

Gospel		Irenaeus	Gospel		Irenaeus
11:1		2.25.3*c*	1:1–5	JD	3.11.1*b*
1:1–2	JD	1.8.5*a*	11:1–14	J	1.9.2*a*
1:1–3	GJ	3.11.8*b*	1:3	J	1.8.5*a*
11:1–3		3.18.1*a*	1:3	Sc	1.22.1*a*
1:1–3	JD	5.18.2*b*	1:3	JD	2.2.5*a*

460

Gospel		Irenaeus	Gospel		Irenaeus
1:3	J	3.8.3a	4:50	L	2.22.3a
1:3		3.21.10a			
1:3	G	4.32.1b	r5:1-9	JD	2.22.3a
s1:6-8	DL	3.11.4a	r5:1-9	L	2.23.2b
1:10-11	J	3.11.2a	5:14	L	4.36.6b
1:10-12	JD	5.18.2b	5:14	L	5.15.2a
1:12		5.18.3b	v5:28-29	L	5.13.1c
v1:13		3.19.2a	v5:39-40	J	4.10.1a
v1:13-14		3.16.2c	5:43	L	5.25.4a
1:14	J	1.8.5c	v5:46	Sc	4.10.1a
1:14	JA	1.9.2c	s5:46-47	J	4.2.3a
1:14	J	3.10.3c			
1:14	G	3.11.2c	r6:1-13	JD	2.22.3a
1:14	DL	3.11.3c	r6:11	L	3.11.5b
1:14		4.20.2b			
1:14	J	5.18.2b	s7:30		3.16.7b
v1:15-16	J	3.10.3b	r7:38-39		5.18.2a
s1:18		3.11.6a			
r1:18		4.6.5c	v8:34	L	3.8.1c
s1:18	G	4.20.6c	8:36	S	3.19.1a
s1:18	L	4.20.11a	s8:44	L	5.22.2c
1:29	J	3.10.3b	8:44	L	5.23.2c
r1:29	J	3.10.3c	8:56	C	4.5.3a
1:47, 49		3.11.6a	r8:56		4.5.5a
v1:50	L	4.9.2a	r8:56		4.7.1a
			8:56-57	L	2.22.6a
r2:1-11	JD	2.22.3a	8:58	W	4.13.4c
r2:1-11		3.11.5a			
2:4	L	3.16.7a	r9:1-42		2.17.9c
v2:19-21	L	5.6.2b	9:3	L	5.15.2b
v2:23	JD	2.22.3a	s9:7		5.15.3c
v2:25		3.9.3c			
			r11:1-57	JD	2.22.3b
v3:5	L	Fr. 35	11:25	L	4.5.2c
3:18-21	L	5.27.2c	r11:35		3.22.2c
v3:36		4.37.5b	r11:39		5.13.1a
			11:43-44		5.13.1b
r4:1-54	JD	2.22.3a			
4:6	JD	3.22.2b	r12:1-19	JD	2.22.3c
r4:14	S	4.36.4a	s12:27	L	1.8.2c
4:35-38	L	4.23.1a	r12:32		4.2.7c
4:37		4.25.3b			
4:41-42		4.2.7a	r13:1-30	JD	2.22.3c

Gospel		Irenaeus	Gospel		Irenaeus
r13:5	W	4.22.1a	v17:24	L	4.14.1c
r14:2		3.19.3c	r18:37		1.6.4b
v14:2	L	5.36.2a			
r14:6	Ap	3.5.1a	19:11		4.18.3c
v14:6–7	L	4.7.3c	19:15	C	4.21.3a
s14:7, 9–10	L	3.13.2a	r19:18	JD	2.22.3c
14:11	L	5.18.1b	r19:34		3.22.2c
r14:16	JA	3.11.9a	r19:34		4.33.2c
14:28	L	2.28.8c	r19:34		4.35.3c
r15:9		3.20.2b	s20:17	L	5.31.1c
v15:15	L	4.13.4b	r20:20	C	5.7.1a
15:16	L	4.14.1b	r20:20	L	5.31.2a
			r20:24		1.18.3c
r16:7	L	3.17.2a	s20:31	JD	3.16.5b
17:5	W	4.14.1a	v21:20	JD	3.1.1c
r17:12	L	2.20.5b	r21:20	J	4.20.11b

A study of the above table offers some considerations which are worthy of special attention as indicating the use which Irenaeus made of the gospel.

1. The student can hardly fail to be struck with the fact that the prologue possessed an apparently undue place in the thinking of Irenaeus. More than one-fourth of the use which he made of the gospel was quotation from the prologue or reference to it. If the influence of the prologue which is to be seen in the mere "coloring" of Irenaeus' language (cf. p. 9) without any specific "reference" were to be taken into account, this disproportionate attention to the prologue would be increased. His large use of the prologue may indicate his estimation of it as compared with other portions of the gospel. Or, he may have employed it so largely because he regarded its statements as conclusive refutations of the theories put forth by his Gnostic opponents.

2. Irenaeus allowed himself a large measure of freedom in making quotations from the gospel. This is particularly true of the quotations outside of the prologue. It suggests that he usually quoted from memory and that most, if not all, of the statements of the gospel to which he appealed were those which he knew sufficiently well to recall without turning to his text. Of the 115 quotations from the gospel, or references to it, which I have credited to Irenaeus, thirty-nine or a full third of these, are merely loose references, while the exact quotations are limited to some twenty-seven different statements, and the inexact ones make up the remainder.

If he did turn to his text at all, it could hardly have been more than occasionally, when, e. g., he wanted such a statement as that of 3:18–21.

3. The reader will observe the great diversity of usage on the part of Irenaeus in acknowledging the source of the material which he employed from the gospel. Even the thirteen classes of acknowledgments which I have enumerated do not exhaust the data, for the thirteenth is a varied datum in itself. Altogether, his usage is very loose. He did not even take the trouble to advise his readers as to whether his "John" was the Baptist, or the Evangelist, so that the references to "John" in 3.10.3 are really to the Baptist, though Irenaeus' general usage would lead one to expect that they were to the Evangelist. The words which the gospel attributes to Jesus are most often said to be the words of "the Lord," but a variation from this usage may occur at any time. There is considerable variety in the way in which a single passage of the gospel is used (e. g., 1:18, or 8:44).

4. A reference to the twenty-first chapter is not certain. The reference to John as the one who leaned on Jesus' breast, in 3.1.1c and 4.20.11b, is better explained, however, from 21:20 than from 13:25 and is to be regarded as a use of 21:20. No reference to the tenth chapter is discoverable. But Clement of Alexandria, only a few years later, quoted this chapter several times and made one clear reference and partial quotation (*Paedag.* 1.5.1a) from the twenty-first chapter. In view of this, it is fair to assume that Irenaeus' gospel contained the tenth chapter and that the reference to John as the one who leaned on Jesus' breast is a reference to the twenty-first chapter.

TABLE II

Showing Irenaeus' use of the gospel from the point of view of the progress of his work. The abbreviations and symbols are the same as in the preceding table.

Irenaeus		Gospel	Irenaeus		Gospel
1.6.4b		r18:37	2.22.3a	JD	r2:1–11
1.8.2c	L	s12:27	2.22.3a	JD	v2:23
1.8.5a	JD	1:1–2	2.22.3a	JD	r4:1–54
1.8.5a	J	1:3	2.22.3a	L	4:50
1.8.5c	J	1:14	2.22.3a	JD	r5:1–9
1.9.2a	J	r1:1–14	2.22.3a	JD	r6:1–13
1.9.2c	JA	1:14	2.22.3b	JD	r11:1–57
1.18.3c		r20:34	2.22.3c	JD	r12:1–19
1.22.1a	Sc	1:3	2.22.3c	JD	r13:1–30
			2.22.3c	JD	r19:18
2.2.5a	JD	1:3	2.22.6a	L	8:56–57
2.17.9c		r9:1–42	2.23.2b	L	r5:1–9
2.20.5b	L	r17:12	2.25.3c		r1:1

HISTORICAL AND LINGUISTIC STUDIES

Irenaeus		Gospel	Irenaeus		Gospel
2.28.8c	L	14:28	4.5.5a		r18:56
			4.6.5c		r11:18
3.1.1c	JD	v21:20	4.7.1a		r8:56
3.5.1a	Ap	r14:6	4.7.3c	L	v14:6-7
3.8.1c	L	v8:34	4.9.2a	L	v1:50
3.8.3a	J	1:3	4.10.1a	J	v5:39-40
3.9.3c		v2:25	4.10.1a	Sc	v5:46
3.10.3b	J	v1:15-16	4.13.4b	L	v15:15
3.10.3b	J	1:29	4.13.4c	W	8:58
3.10.3c	J	1:14	4.14.1a	W	17:5
3.10.3c	J	r1:29	4.14.1b	L	15:16
3.11.1b	JD	1:1-5	4.14.1c	L	v17:24
3.11.2a	J	1:10-11	4.18.3c		19:11
3.11.2c	G	1:14	4.20.2b		1:14
3.11.3c	DL	1:14	4.20.6c	G	s1:18
3.11.4a	DL	s1:6-8	4.20.11a	L	s1:18
3.11.5a		r2:1-11	4.20.11b	J	r21:20
3.11.5b	L	r6:11	4.21.3a	C	19:15
3.11.6a		s1:18	4.22.1a	W	r13:5
3.11.6a		1:47, 49	4.23.1a	L	4:35-38
3.11.8b	GJ	1:1-3	4.25.3b		4:37
3.11.9a	JA	r14:16	4.32.1b	G	1:3
3.13.2a	L	s14:7, 9-10	4.33.2c		r19:34
3.16.2c		v1:13-14	4.35.3c		r19:34
3.16.5b	JD	s20:31	4.36.4a	S	r4:14
3.16.7a	L	2:4	4.36.6b	L	5:14
3.16.7b		s7:30	4.37.5b		v3:36
3.17.2a	L	r16:7			
3.18.1a		r1:1-3	5.6.2b	L	v2:19-21
3.19.1a	S	8:36	5.7.1a	C	r20:20
3.19.2a		v1:13	5.13.1a		r11:39
3.19.3c		r14:2	5.13.1b		11:43-44
3.20.2b		r15:9	5.13.1c	L	v5:28-29
3.21.10a		1:3	5.15.2a	L	5:14
3.22.2b	JD	4:6	5.15.2b	L	9:3
3.22.2c		r11:35	5.15.3c		s9:7
3.22.2c		r19:34	5.18.1b	L	14:11
			5.18.2a		r7:38-39
4.2.3a	J	s5:46-47	5.18.2b	JD	1:1-3
4.2.7a		4:41-42	5.18.2b	JD	1:10-12
4.2.7c		r12:32	5.18.2b	J	1:14
4.5.2c	L	11:25	5.18.3b		1:12
4.5.3a	L	8:56	5.22.2c	L	s8:44

464

IRENAEUS TESTIMONY TO THE FOURTH GOSPEL   15

Irenaeus		Gospel	Irenaeus		Gospel
5.23.2c	L	8:44	5.31.2a	L	120:20
5.25.4a	L	5:43	5.36.2a	L	VI4:2
5.27.2c	L	3:18–21			
5.31.1c	L	s20:17	Fr. 35	L	v3:5

A study of this second table is hardly less suggestive than that of the preceding.

1. From it one might infer that Irenaeus had neglected the use of the gospel in the early portion of his work, for only twelve of the chapters of his entire first two books have even a reference to the gospel. This neglect is merely apparent, however, not real. In his first book Irenaeus was only stating the teachings of his opponents preparatory to making a criticism of them, and even the slight use which he made of the gospel was not strictly in accord with the plan which he outlined for himself. In his second book he presented his own more philosophical criticism of the Gnostics, and this did not properly allow a considerable use of the gospel. Not till the beginning of his third book did his general scheme make it appropriate for him to appeal largely to the Scriptures.

2. The summary of the contents of the gospel in 2.22.3 is worthy of special attention. In discussing the chronology of Jesus' life, Irenaeus referred to those parts of the gospel which seemed to him to prove that the ministry of Jesus extended over more than a year. His reference becomes a kind of epitome of the contents of the gospel and indicates, in compact form, the contents of the gospel as he had it. A glance at the gospel references, in the table, opposite to 2.22.3 gives considerable reason to infer, from this reference alone, that Irenaeus had before him chaps. 2–19 inclusive of our gospel.

3. In the preceding table, the variety of abbreviations for the authorities to whom Irenaeus attributed the statements of the gospel indicated the looseness of his usage. Here this variety offers a different suggestion. The reader will observe a change of usage during the progress of the work. In the early portion of his discussion Irenaeus attributed his quotations and references chiefly to "John," or to "John, the disciple of the Lord." Later there is more variety, as though his thought of the source of the gospel statements was changing and becoming unstable. In Book 5 he attributed the statements of the gospel almost entirely to "the Lord." The simplest conclusion is that his conception of Jesus had developed in the course of the composition of his apology and manifested itself in the selection of the titles for his authorities. Such a development in his thought was natural enough, for the summaries at the beginning and close of his different books

make it probable that the composition extended over some months at least, perhaps over a longer period; he may even have published the work in instalments, for he was evidently eager to offset the Gnostic teachings as early as possible. If the work did thus cover an extended period, he would easily come to feel that the gospel was more directly the product of Jesus himself, not as to its writing, but as to its source and authority.

From the extent of Irenaeus' use of the fourth gospel, as seen in the above varied ways, we are warranted in concluding that he possessed substantially the same gospel which has come down to us, and that his text was not very different from the one which we read.

CHAPTER II

THE AUTHOR OF THE FOURTH GOSPEL FOR IRENAEUS

The large use which Irenaeus made of the fourth gospel leaves no doubt that he was much interested in the material which the gospel gave to him. This gospel was one of the chief authorities to which he appealed. If he did not think it superior to other scriptures to which he turned in support of his arguments, he at least did not regard it as inferior to others. It is of interest and of importance, therefore, to know what Irenaeus thought of the authorship of the fourth gospel. Anticipations of this have already appeared in the titles which the two tables present for Irenaeus' authorities in referring to the gospel. The following statements will put the matter into more definite form.

1. For Irenaeus, the fourth gospel was the work of John of Asia of late apostolic times, apostolic times extending, for him, as far as the days of Trajan (2.22.5*c*; 3.3.4*c*).

The evidence for this statement is so ample that there is little need to discuss it. Reference to the above tables is all that is required to warrant it. From those it is seen that about one-fourth of the references to the gospel were attributed, in one form of expression or another, to John. Sometimes the quotation or reference was attributed to John without any further identification of the person of whom he thought. Frequently the author of the gospel was John, "the disciple of the Lord." Again he was simply "the disciple of the Lord," but the context makes it certain that the author so designated was this same John. The very freedom which Irenaeus felt in his reference to the gospel is an indirect assurance of his certainty concerning the author.

2. Aside from John the Baptist and John Mark, Irenaeus recognized only one John of apostolic times.

John Mark is mentioned in 3.14.1*a*, but with a clear recognition that he was a different person from the John of whom Irenaeus thought as the author of the gospel. John the Baptist is named, or the language which the gospels attribute to him is quoted as his, several times (e. g., 1.3.5*b*; 1.30.12*b*; 3.10.3*a*; 4.4.3*b*; 5.17.4*b*). In some instances, as already pointed out (p. 13), Irenaeus did not concern himself to inform his readers whether he was speaking of the Baptist, or the Evangelist. In 4.4.3*b* he chose to say that the John he was introducing was the Baptist, even though he had referred to him simply as John only a few lines earlier on his page. No sufficient reason for this appears. Perhaps it was due to the general habit of looseness of expression which is a characteristic of Irenaeus' style and is the outcome of looseness of thought. At the same time, to anyone who examines the references in their contexts, it is evident that Irenaeus was never in doubt as to whether John the Baptist was a different man from the author of the gospel.

This is an important point. It limits at once the possibilities as to the author of the fourth gospel for Irenaeus. For him, the author of the gospel was the one John of New Testament times other than John the Baptist and John Mark.

3. This John of Asia who was, for Irenaeus, the writer of the fourth gospel, was not only "the disciple of the Lord," but also an "apostle."

Those who have discussed the testimony of Irenaeus have sometimes minimized, or even entirely overlooked, this point. It is important, therefore, that the meaning of Irenaeus' language be made clear, and a single passage seems sufficient to put the matter beyond question. It is that in 1.9.2b, where Irenaeus declared that the interpretation of the fourth gospel which his opponents had offered would make John refer to "the primary ogdoad, in which there was as yet no Jesus, and no Christ, the teacher of John. But that the apostle did not so speak .... he himself has made evident; for he declares, 'And the word was made flesh and dwelt among us.'" It is true, of course, that this does not give the phrase for which some have asked, "John, the Apostle," or "John, the son of Zebedee." But the reader of the statement in its context, if not in the quotation, can hardly find the language less definite. The expression is an incidental one, but it can hardly mean that Irenaeus had in mind any other than the apostle John, the son of Zebedee.

A passage from the third book is hardly less decisive. At the close of 3.3.4, Irenaeus wrote: "The church in Ephesus, founded by Paul, and having John remaining among them permanently until the times of Trajan, is a true witness of the traditions of the apostles." The obvious meaning of this statement is that, for Irenaeus, the John of Asia was an apostle. Taken with the point which has been made above—that Irenaeus recognized only one John of apostolic days other than John the Baptist and John Mark—the statement means that the writer of the gospel was an apostle. The passage in 2.22.5c contains similar language and gives the same conclusion.

Again, in 3.5.1a, Irenaeus referred to "those apostles who did also write the gospel .... pointing out that our Lord Jesus Christ is the truth."

This is manifestly a reference to John 14:6, and makes the author of the statement an apostle. This apostle must have been John, for John was Irenaeus' author of the fourth gospel.

Four other passages yield essentially the same evidence, though not in so specific form. In 3.11.9*b* Irenaeus urged that the Valentinian writing which the Valentinians called "The Gospel of Truth" did not at all agree with "the gospels of the apostles." Thus, by the use of the plural, "the apostles," two at least of the evangelists were made apostles, one of whom, for Irenaeus, is most naturally thought of as the fourth. In 3.12.5*a* the Peter and John who are described in the fourth chapter of Acts are said to have returned "*ad reliquos co-apostolos.*" This John, according to Acts, is evidently the apostle, and Irenaeus could hardly have thought of him differently. From the close of 3.16.1 we learn that Irenaeus judged it necessary to take into account "the entire mind of the apostles," which he made to include the mind of John as well as of Matthew and others. Later (3.21.3*c*), he insisted that the LXX translation harmonized with the traditions of "the apostles; for Peter, and John, and Matthew, and Paul, and the rest successively," followed that translation.

Remembering that John the disciple was, for Irenaeus, the writer of the gospel, Irenaeus' letter to Victor (Eus.*H.E.*5.24) gives a specific statement that the author of the gospel was an apostle. Irenaeus wrote that Polycarp would not forego his custom of observing Easter because he had received it from John and "other apostles." John is thus described, indirectly, as an apostle.

This cumulation of evidence places Irenaeus' opinion beyond doubt. The author of the fourth gospel was as certainly an apostle for him as though he had taken a page, to state, argue, and prove the point. He would have been astonished if he could have known that any reader would ever think otherwise. One can hardly believe that those who have been in doubt about the matter have read Irenaeus.[1]

---

[1] E. g., H. L. Jackson, *The Fourth Gospel and Some Recent German Criticism,* 1906, p. 45: "The decisive word 'apostle' is missing." Cf. especially the hesitation of Swete, *The Apocalypse of St. John,* 1906, p. clxxiv: "No second-century testimony, except that of the Leucian Acts, excludes the hypothesis that the John who lived in Asia and wrote the Apocalypse [and as certainly, substantially, the gospel, according to Swete] was the Elder, or compels us to believe that John the Apostle ever resided in Asia. Moreover, it is certainly remarkable that in so many of the earliest references to him John of Asia is called 'the disciple,' and not, expressly at least, the Apostle." C. A. Scott, in reviewing Swete's work for *The Expositor* (January, 1907, p. 45) blindly follows in the same direction, and speaks of "Irenaeus' steady refraining from calling 'John' an apostle."

Though the conclusion is so evident and convincing, one may still ask why Irenaeus never used the phrase, "John, the apostle." The answer is an easy one for those who have so read Irenaeus as to catch his spirit and to discover the principles which guided him in the choice of expressions. Such readers discover that the terminology of Irenaeus was that of the New Testament. Now, the New Testament usually introduces a person by name without any further designation. This is the New Testament usage concerning John, except that he is distinguished as the brother of James; and it accounts for the usage of Irenaeus, for John, "the apostle," is not a New Testament expression. But "disciple" is New Testament language. In the gospels, "disciple" is the ordinary word, "apostle" being very uncommon as compared with it. From the New Testament we could not expect to get "John, the apostle." Still further, "*the* disciple," in the singular, as a title for a person, is an expression found in the fourth gospel only.[1] To be sure, the expression, "the disciple of the Lord" is not found in the gospel. On the other hand, Irenaeus did not use the name "Jesus" alone, but, as has been pointed out above (p. 15), he spoke frequently of "the Lord."[2] It was a very natural thing, then, for Irenaeus to retain "the disciple," but to change "of Jesus" into "of the Lord." With this slight change, the gospel itself offered a unique title for its author, while to have spoken of him, either as an author or otherwise, as "apostle," would have been to disregard entirely the usage which the New Testament gave. When he was referred to as an apostle, it was only incidentally.

This conclusion naturally raises the question: What was Irenaeus' general use of the word "apostle"? The material offered in reply is interesting indeed. It shows not only his thought of an "apostle," but also his attitude to the apostolic age as a whole.

According to his statement in 3.11.4c, he regarded John the Baptist as an apostle. The Latin reads: "*Ipse* [John the Baptist] *et prophetae et apostoli locum habuerit.*" The genitive with "*locum*" might seem to be a careful method of avoiding the statement that John was an apostle, of saying only that John was a kind of vice-apostle. But this is to attribute to Irenaeus a carefulness of language which he never observed. Moreover, such an interpretation proves too much. If it proves that John was only a vice-apostle, it proves that he was only a vice-prophet, for the con-

---

[1] See John 18:15, 16; 19:26, 27; 20:2, 3, 4, 8; 21:7, 20, 23, 24; in some of which the Greek shows the article as the English cannot.

[2] See *Heresies* 2.22 for an extended example of his usage, the more striking because he is there discussing Jesus' age, which would, if any topic would, lead him to use the name Jesus.

struction is the same for both words. But Irenaeus had just made him a prophet by comparing him with "the other prophets." Accordingly, he intended the phrase to mean that John was an apostle as well as a prophet.

A statement at the close of 3.11.9 is even more inclusive. Irenaeus had just discussed, in order, the evidence from the four gospels. He continued: "*Examinata igitur sententia eorum qui nobis tradiderunt evangelium, ... veniamus et ad reliquos apostolos.*" This makes Mark and Luke apostles, for it is evident that Irenaeus had these men in mind, rather than Peter and Paul—whom he had previously (3.1.1) made sources, for Mark and Luke respectively, of the second and third gospels—because he proceeded at once to discuss Peter as one of the "remaining apostles." These latter also are interesting, for they include not only Peter, but John (3.12.3a), Philip (3.12.8a), Stephen (3.12.10a), and Barnabas (3.12.15c), as though Irenaeus was writing with Acts before him and arranging the material about these prominent persons who are mentioned in the book. This accounts for the repetition of testimony from John. And he made the matter still more definite when he introduced his summary of the entire argument with the statement: "*Sic apostoli .... religiose agebant.*" As though to clinch the point—yet to do so never occurred to him—he later (3.21.4a) quoted Matt. 1:18 and Luke 1:35 together as statements which "*ipsi* [the apostles] *testificantur.*"[1]

Indeed, the apostles, for Irenaeus, were not limited to such a list as that which has just been given. He thought of all the Christian men of the apostolic days, at least all the prominent ones, as essentially apostles. This statement cannot be proved as definitely as the several persons named above have been proved to have been, for Irenaeus, apostles, but it is implied in such expressions as the following: "This tradition from the apostles" (2.9.1c); that Soter was the twelfth bishop of Rome "from the apostles .... from the apostles till now" (3.3.3c); "the tradition from the apostles" (3.5.1a); "the succession from the apostles" (4.26.2a); "the doctrine of the apostles and the ancient constitution of the church" (4.33.8a); "all these [Irenaeus' opponents] are of much later date than the bishops to whom the apostles committed the churches .... the sure tradition from the apostles" (5.20.1a, b).

Accordingly, when Irenaeus spoke of a man as an "apostle," that in itself means merely that the man belonged to the first century. The term

---

[1] Cf. Monnier, *La notion de l'apostolat*, 1903, p. 362: "L'apostolat de Paul et des Douze n'est pas exclusif d'un apostolat plus étendu. Irénée invoque, à l'appui des Évangiles, le témoignage du *reste des apôtres* (3.11.9e). Il identifie donc les Évangélistes avec les Apôtres. Barnabas aussi est un apôtre."

becomes more definite only through a limitation by other data which he offers, as e. g., in the case of John the author of the gospel, who, in the manner indicated above, is not only distinguished from John the Baptist and John Mark (p. 17), but is also found to be clearly an apostle (pp. 18, 19).

"*Sacerdotes autem sunt omnes Domini apostoli*" in 4.8.3*b* appears to indicate an even looser use of the word "apostle," as though apostles were not confined to the first century. But perhaps Irenaeus did not mean that. The context can hardly be said to make the time of the verb certain. There is less reason for pressing the point in either direction because we have only the Latin. The Greek which Irenaeus wrote may have given the passage a different coloring.

A statement of Irenaeus in 3.12.15*c* further illustrates his attitude to the apostolic age as a whole. Inasmuch as it is usually misinterpreted and made to create a prejudice against his testimony to the fourth gospel, its consideration here will serve a twofold purpose. It is the parenthetical statement, "*ubique enim simul cum eo adsistentes inveniuntur Petrus et Iacobus et Ioannes,*" in which the reference to James, directly after Irenaeus had been speaking of James the brother of Jesus and without anything to differentiate them, is usually understood to be a manifest confusion of the two men. But the language of Irenaeus, when rightly understood, does not involve such a conclusion. The key to the language is to be found in what has been said above (p. 20) of the way in which Irenaeus adopted New Testament phraseology. The combination, "Peter, James, and John," was a New Testament expression of special prominence and significance. At this point of his discussion it served Irenaeus admirably. He was appealing to what he regarded as general Judaeo-Christian custom in the apostolic age concerning eating with gentiles. This is seen from the form of his concluding statement: "*Sic apostoli, quos universi actus et universae doctrinae Dominus testes fecit . . . . religiose agebant.*" It is seen also in the tenor of the entire section. Accordingly, he could include James the brother of John as proof of his argument; and the familiar gospel phrase was used without stopping to consider that, in its context, it could be misunderstood. It was not Irenaeus' nature or custom to stop to consider such possibilities of misunderstanding. To fail to recognize this is to do Irenaeus much injustice.

Aside from the case of 4.8.3*b* above, therefore, and perhaps inclusive of it, the language of Irenaeus implies that he thought of the apostles as men belonging to the first century only and as forming a group of Christians by themselves. They occupied this unique position, however, not because they belonged to the circle of the twelve, or of the twelve and Paul, but because they had the privilege of a peculiar relation to Jesus. Many of them had associated with him. Others (especially Mark and Luke) had been honored with the position of writing of his life and mission. Others (e. g., Stephen, Philip, and Barnabas) had rendered special service appropriate to the period. One, John, who had been most intimately associated with Jesus, had lived to remarkably advanced years and preserved the character of the age. While he remained, the "apostolic" age continued; when he died that age passed away. In view of all this, the heritage which came from the age of the apostles was unique and was worthy of preeminent consideration, whether this heritage came in written form or through personal tradition. Irenaeus did not think of criticizing it, if it was well attested. That which was assured to have come from the apostles was authoritative.

4. While it must be admitted, therefore, that the word "apostle" applied by Irenaeus to the John whom he recognized as author of the gospel would not, of itself, identify him as the son of Zebedee, yet it remains true that "apostle" usually meant for him what it means in the New Testament. Accordingly, when we take into account that he recognized only one John other than John the Baptist and John Mark and that this one John, on the basis of Irenaeus' own testimony rightly understood, was an "apostle," the conditions which his testimony as a whole imposes are satisfied only by the conclusion that the son of Zebedee was, for Irenaeus, the author of the fourth gospel.

CHAPTER III

THE VALUE OF THE IRENAEUS TESTIMONY FOR US

We have seen that Irenaeus thought of the son of Zebedee as the author of the fourth gospel. His certainty concerning the authorship of the gospel, however, cannot be accepted as affording the same certainty for us. Even with all his assurance, Irenaeus may have been led into error. His work was not the result of critical investigation, at least in the sense in which we now think of critical investigation, and we cannot accept his confident statements at their face value, unless we have discovered that they are worth that. We know that he made a mistake concerning the third gospel, for he wrote that Luke, as "the companion of Paul, recorded in a book the gospel preached by him" (3.1.1c). The student of the synoptic gospels at the present time does not understand that Luke gained the material for his gospel from Paul. Irenaeus may have made a mistake concerning the composition of the fourth gospel also. The material which he transmitted to us must be critically examined, therefore, that we may discover how well founded his assurance was.

This material, as it bears upon the fourth gospel, is presented in what he wrote of his relation to Polycarp, to the presbyters, and to Papias. We may consider that concerning Polycarp first. It is extant in three significant passages from Irenaeus' writings. These are: His letter to Victor, bishop of Rome, preserved by Eusebius ($H.E.$ 5.24); a letter to Florinus, also preserved by Eusebius ($H.E.$ 5.20); and *Heresies* 3.3.4.

The significant phrases of Eusebius' introduction to the letter to Victor and of the letter itself, for this study, are as follows: Ἐν οἷς [the different ones who wrote to Victor] καὶ ὁ Εἰρηναῖος ἐκ προσώπου ὧν ἡγεῖτο κατὰ τὴν Γαλλίαν ἀδελφῶν . . . . ἐπιλέγων· . . . . Καὶ τοιαύτη μὲν ποικιλία τῶν ἐπιτηρούντων, οὐ νῦν ἐφ' ἡμῶν γεγονυῖα, ἀλλὰ καὶ πολὺ πρότερον ἐπὶ τῶν πρὸ ἡμῶν . . . . καὶ οὐδὲν ἔλαττον πάντες οὗτοι εἰρήνευσάν τε, καὶ εἰρηνεύομεν πρὸς ἀλλήλους . . . . καὶ τοῦ μακαρίου Πολυκάρπου ἐπιδημήσαντος ἐν Ῥώμῃ ἐπὶ Ἀνικήτου . . . . εὐθὺς εἰρήνευσαν . . . . οὔτε γὰρ ὁ Ἀνίκητος τὸν Πολύκαρπον πεῖσαι ἐδύνατο μὴ τηρεῖν ἅτε μετὰ Ἰωάννου τοῦ μαθητοῦ κυρίου ἡμῶν καὶ λοιπῶν ἀποστόλων, οἷς συνδιέτριψεν, ἀεὶ τετηρηκότα· οὔτε μὴν ὁ Πολύκαρπος τὸν Ἀνίκητον ἔπεισε τηρεῖν. . . . . The language warrants the following statements concerning the source and trustworthiness of the testimony.

1. The letter was written, on behalf of the Christians in Gaul, to Victor

as the bishop of the church in Rome. It was evidently a letter which was intended to be of a public nature, an "open letter," so that it was expected to be subject to criticism. It became public property and stood the test of criticism well enough to be regarded as valuable for preservation.

2. From the letter we learn that Polycarp was in Rome in the time of Anicetus (who was bishop of Rome about 154 to 156). One of the leading topics of conversation at that time was the observance of Easter. In this discussion Polycarp maintained his position, because he could say that his custom of observance rested on the custom of "John, the disciple of our Lord, and the rest of the apostles," with whom he had observed it.

3. In this letter Irenaeus asserted that, in spite of the difference between the Roman Christians and those of Asia as to the observance of Easter, there had been fellowship and peace between them at the time of which he was speaking, i. e., at a little past the middle of the second century. The Roman Christians in the time of Irenaeus were in a position to know whether such had been the situation in the time of Anicetus, only thirty or forty years before. The memory of some of the older ones could have bridged the time with substantial accuracy, and documents of one kind or another were almost certainly in existence bearing on a topic which was regarded as so important as that of Easter and the earlier relations between Asia and Rome. Irenaeus' appeal to Victor must have been well founded, and we are led to conclude that the situation at the middle of the second century was substantially that which Irenaeus described toward the close of the century.

4. Such a presentation of the question in dispute as Irenaeus made in this letter implies that he was independently and directly well informed as to the situation in Asia at the time of Anicetus. Otherwise he could not have written to Rome as he did. If he had gotten his information merely through Rome, Rome could have replied that his argument had no value for her, since she was already in possession of as much information as he was. At most his letter could only have been an appeal, and he would naturally have made such an appeal on the basis of reference to what he had received from Rome. But the letter contains no such reference. Rather it proceeds in an independent manner. The dispute had not arisen within the times in which he was living, he said, but long before; and the statement implies that he had known of the entire history of the dispute independently of his relations with Rome. He could easily have known this, of course, since close communication between the East and the West is well known to have been an ordinary event of the times.[1]

[1] That his letter to Victor did not accomplish the purpose for which it was sent is

5. The fact that the dispute had arisen long before the time of Irenaeus implies that it had been under discussion long enough to bring out all the facts in the case and make them well known. As a corollary, the statement of Irenaeus implies that an error of claim would easily have been recognized and set aside. There were plenty of well-recognized data, and Irenaeus naturally confined himself to them.

6. Putting all this material together, it is seen that the testimony of Irenaeus in this letter is not a single testimony from the last part of the second century. Instead, it is the generally accepted understanding of conditions by the Christians of the middle of the second century, both in Rome, in Asia, and in Gaul.

7. But this takes the testimony, at least as much of it as came from Polycarp, back to his lifetime and activity, and makes it substantially his testimony. We have in this letter a presentation of some of the affairs of Asia as Polycarp had been familiar with them during his long life in the midst of Asian events.

8. Inasmuch as Polycarp was a man some thirty years of age at the close of the first century, we are here given the testimony of a man who was fully conversant with events and opinions of that time, and the testimony which we are considering is seen to be the testimony of the close of the first century.

The letter to Florinus (Eus. *H.E.* 5.20) may now be examined in a similar way. Florinus had renounced some views which Irenaeus regarded as essential to Christian teaching, and Irenaeus wrote in protest. The portions of the letter which bear on the worth of the testimony and its significance for the fourth gospel are as follows: Ταῦτα τὰ δόγματα οἱ πρὸ ἡμῶν πρεσβύτεροι, οἱ καὶ τοῖς ἀποστόλοις συμφοιτήσαντες, οὐ παρέδωκάν σοι. Εἶδον γάρ σε, παῖς ὢν ἔτι, ἐν τῇ κάτω Ἀσίᾳ παρὰ τῷ Πολυκάρπῳ . . . . πειρώμενον εὐδοκιμεῖν παρ' αὐτῷ. Μᾶλλον γὰρ τὰ τότε διαμνημονεύω τῶν ἔναγχος γινομένων . . . . ὥστε με δύνασθαι εἰπεῖν καὶ τὸν τόπον ἐν ᾧ καθεζόμενος διελέγετο ὁ μακάριος Πολύκαρπος, καὶ τὰς προόδους αὐτοῦ καὶ τὰς εἰσόδους καὶ τὸν χαρακτῆρα τοῦ βίου καὶ τὴν τοῦ σώματος ἰδέαν καὶ τὰς διαλέξεις ἃς ἐποιεῖτο πρὸς τὸ πλῆθος, καὶ τὴν μετὰ Ἰωάννου συναστροφὴν ὡς ἀπήγγελλε, καὶ τὴν τῶν λοιπῶν τῶν ἑωρακότων τὸν Κύριον, καὶ ὡς ἀπεμνημόνευε τοὺς λόγους αὐτῶν· καὶ περὶ τοῦ Κυρίου τίνα ἦν ἃ παρ' ἐκείνων ἀκηκόει, καὶ περὶ τῶν δυνάμεων αὐτοῦ, καὶ

not a serious objection to my argument, for the entire account of the affair, as given by Eusebius, indicates that Victor acted arbitrarily, perhaps for ecclesiastical purposes, rather than in the spirit which had prevailed in the time of Anicetus. Though Eusebius did not take sides in the matter, it is evident that he felt the strength of the Asian claim, as may be seen by his various comments throughout the chapter.

περὶ τῆς διδασκαλίας, ὡς παρὰ τῶν αὐτοπτῶν τῆς ζωῆς τοῦ λόγου παρειληφὼς ὁ Πολύκαρπος, ἀπήγγελλε πάντα σύμφωνα ταῖς γραφαῖς. Ταῦτα .... ἤκουον. .... Καὶ δύναμαι διαμαρτύρασθαι .... ὅτι εἴτι τοιοῦτον ἀκηκόει ἐκεῖνος ὁ μακάριος πρεσβύτερος .... πεφεύγοι ἂν .... Καὶ ἐκ τῶν ἐπιστολῶν δὲ αὐτοῦ, ὧν ἐπέστειλεν ἤτοι ταῖς γειτνιώσαις ἐκκλησίαις ἐπιστηρίζων αὐτάς, ἢ τῶν ἀδελφῶν τισὶ νουθετῶν αὐτοὺς καὶ προτρεπόμενος, δύναται φανερωθῆναι. This is a vivid and detailed account of a situation, and its trustworthiness is of prime importance. As to what this trustworthiness is, the letter justifies the following statements:

1. Irenaeus was writing to a man who was somewhat older than himself. They had both lived in Asia in early life and had known each other there. Apparently Florinus had remained in Asia after Irenaeus had removed to Europe. Whether he had, or had not, he had been at least a young man as early as the middle of the second century.[1] He had thus been in a position to know the situation in Asia at that time. Because of this personal knowledge which Florinus had, Irenaeus sought to dissuade him from a course of thought and action which that early knowledge and the training from it, according to Irenaeus, fully condemned. The argument of Irenaeus was based on the intimate relations which had existed between Florinus and Polycarp and on Irenaeus' knowledge of those relations to a sufficient extent to be certain of what they were. The facts must have been substantially as Irenaeus stated them. Otherwise he would have made himself ridiculous before Florinus and merely have played into the hand of his opponent.[2]

2. This trustworthy letter traces many of its claims to Polycarp. The fundamental ones for determining the relation of Irenaeus to the fourth gospel are of that kind. The material offered by the letter, therefore, is not so much the testimony of Irenaeus as it is the testimony of Polycarp, for Irenaeus rested his case on the claim that Florinus had received these things from Polycarp and recognized that he had so received them. If this had not been substantially the situation, Irenaeus' letter would have been of trifling worth and probably of only temporary interest.

[1] I am assuming the chronology of Harnack, according to which Irenaeus was born probably as early as 135, and may have been born earlier.

[2] It may be objected that the letter must have been such that Florinus could use it against Irenaeus, or Florinus would have suppressed it. But to say that is to overlook the fact that the contents of the letter would be used in other ways. If Florinus attempted to suppress it, such an action would only lead to a re-writing of the substance of the letter. Most probably the letter originally was an open communication, and we must believe its presentation of affairs for the middle of the second century to have been essentially correct.

3. Here, then, as in the case of the letter to Victor, we discover that the testimony which we gain from Irenaeus is that which comes from Polycarp and reaches back to the close of the first century. Perhaps the early date of the testimony is somewhat more certain in this case than it was in the other, for Florinus was in a better position to know Asia and its thought at the middle of the second century than any of the Roman Christians were. At least, we do not know that Victor, or any of those in Rome in his time, had lived in Asia at the middle of the century as Florinus had. If Victor had lived there in his early life, Irenaeus would have been likely to refer to the fact in the letter to him, just as he referred to Florinus' life there. Florinus had been closely associated with Polycarp, and what Florinus recognized as coming from Polycarp was well authenticated.

4. There is one important datum in this letter which is not brought out into the same relief in the letter to Victor. It is the fact that one link made the connection between Florinus and Irenaeus, on the one hand, and the apostles on the other. The link is perhaps implicit in the letter to Victor, but it has not the certainty there which appears here. Here it is expressly said that Polycarp and other presbyters were associated with the apostles and later were associated with Florinus. The significance of this is twofold: it introduces the word "presbyter," and thus shows a point of contact with the other presbyter testimony, which will be considered later; and, more important, it means that Florinus recognized that the testimony which he had received from Polycarp he had received at first hand. He knew whether Polycarp had spoken to him of things which Polycarp had received from John and other apostles. Irenaeus and Florinus both knew whether communication had passed between them concerning the things which Florinus had received from Polycarp. When Irenaeus appealed to Florinus, therefore, he did it assuming a background created by such communication. If we had the letter entire, we should probably find in the first part of it some reference to such communication.

Irenaeus' statements concerning Polycarp in *Heresies* 3.3.4 do not add very materially to the data already found in these two letters, as far as the questions raised by the fourth gospel are concerned. That they do not is natural, or even an indirect evidence of the spontaneity and genuineness of both. The discussion here is a general one, most of the readers of which would not be in a position to verify details concerning Polycarp. Therefore Irenaeus did not attempt to enter into details. A comprehensive statement served his purpose.

There are two phrases in the passage, however, that may be worth noting. One of these is the statement that Polycarp was bishop of the

·church in Smyrna. This is of some importance because it emphasizes the fact that he occupied an important place in Asia and was therefore in a position to know well of Asian men and affairs.

A more important assertion, perhaps, is, that the things of which Irenaeus wrote were attested by all the churches of Asia and by the (episcopal) successors of Polycarp to Irenaeus' own day. A statement like this would soon be read in Asia, and some of the Christians there would be able to know whether the statement was correct. Irenaeus wrote with the knowledge that this would occur. He must have had good authority for the assertion. Thus the statement becomes another assurance that Irenaeus was so fully in communication with Asia that he could appeal directly to Asian conditions.

Altogether, the letter to Victor, the letter to Florinus, and the passage in the *Heresies* are in accord, at the same time that they give sufficiently different details to show that they were spontaneous statements, called out by different sets of conditions. Their agreements and, at the same time, their supplementary nature corroborate their trustworthiness which has been assured on independent grounds. They tell us of the place which Polycarp and those associated with him occupied at the close of the first century, and they convey an account of some of the most important things which were then being said.

Especially, these writings tell us of the Asian John and of what Asia thought of Johannine writings. What is thus preserved for us concerning John and the Johannine writings we are now in a position to see, no longer on the basis of testimony from the close of the second century alone, but also on the assurance of that testimony traced back to the close of the first century and verified as the testimony of that earlier time. The findings from the testimony may be summed up as follows:

I. John the disciple is now an apostle on the authority of Polycarp, as the following considerations taken together show.

Both the letter to Victor and that to Florinus refer to the way in which Polycarp used to speak of John the disciple of Jesus. In the letter to Victor Polycarp made this John specifically an apostle. There is no discussion in either of the letters as to whether the John so mentioned was an apostle; that he was one of the twelve apostles of Jesus appears to have been taken for granted. Whether he was such an apostle or not Polycarp had been in a position to know. The John so mentioned, as Harnack has pointed out (*Chron.* I, 656), was a man of marked distinction. At the same time, as we have already seen (chap. ii), Irenaeus, whose thought in the letters before us, as we have further seen, was the testimony of Polycarp, knew the celebrated John of Asia only as the son of Zebedee. All these several data are explained, if Florinus, the Christians in Rome, Irenaeus, and those who were associated with these men learned from Polycarp that he had been associated in Asia Minor with the son of Zebedee and did not learn from him of any other eminent John. It is natural to conclude, therefore, that the celebrated John of Asia was the son of Zebedee.[1]

[1] The argument of de Boor (*Texte und Untersuchungen*, V, 2) to the effect that the death of John the son of Zebedee occurred in Palestine at about the middle of the first century does not rest upon such early and trustworthy testimony as that of Polycarp through Irenaeus, which has led to the conclusion that John resided in Asia Minor till near the close of the century. Even the fragments of Georgius Hamartolus and Philippus Sidetes, though they both say that John suffered death at the hands of Jews, do not agree in the significant parts of the statement; and neither one locates the death of John in Palestine. These fragments, therefore, when all the evidence is taken into account, are unsatisfactory evidence for the early martyrdom of John. At the same time, their existence at a later period may be readily explained; they are the variant traditions, it would seem, which developed during the later decades, variants which naturally appeared as the tradition became separated from those who had been personally associated with apostolic leaders.

The remainder of the possible evidence for the death of John in Palestine at an early date is still less convincing. Of this evidence, Mark 10:39 and the parallel account in Matthew (20:22) are perhaps the best, but the arguments from the statements (e. g., that of Bacon on "The Martyr Apostles" in *The Expositor* for September, 1907) lack cogency. In Mark the tenses of the significant verbs are probably sufficient alone to indicate that the second evangelist did not understand Jesus' language to refer to martyrdom, for Jesus is made to speak of the cup which "I am drinking" and the baptism with which "I am being baptized," both verbs being presents and probably progressive presents. Accordingly, the cup of which Jesus was thinking for himself, and the one which he predicted for James and John, was one which was to be drunk by living rather than by dying; if its outcome should prove to be death, that was merely incidental. The emphatic element in the language of Mark is that James and John must be prepared to do in the future what Jesus was doing at the time he was speaking; they must be prepared to live as he was living, whatever might be the result. In Matthew the verb does appear to indicate that the evangelist put Jesus' cup beyond the time when Jesus was speaking, though μέλλω does not always have the future idea and does not necessarily have it here. Let us assume, however, that it is future in this case. Then the Matthew change of the Mark material might give a considerable probability that John became a martyr after the second gospel was written but before the composition of the first, if, at the same time, we had no other evidence bearing on the question. But, when the evidence from Polycarp is taken into account, we are under obligation to see whether the first evangelist may have been led by some other motive than the intervening death of John to modify the Mark material. One such motive may have been that, as he mentioned only a "cup," but not a "baptism," so he may have concentrated his thought on the death of James and interpreted Jesus' statement accordingly. Or, he may have been controlled by some other motive, the evidence of which we do not possess. Bacon's finding that "the disciple

II. The testimony from Polycarp offers suggestive material concerning the Johannine writings as well as concerning the Asian John. In the letter to Florinus, from which quotation has been made above (p. 26), there occurs the following statement: ὁ Πολύκαρπος ἀπήγγελλε πάντα σύμφωνα ταῖς γραφαῖς. The πάντα, as a reading of the letter shows, were the details of the stories which Polycarp used to relate concerning

whom Jesus loved" was Paul (*The Expositor*, October, 1907) is highly ingenious, but not convincing. His discussion probably merely carries appreciation of the actual symbolism of the New Testament to an absurdity.

The omission of John's name from the letters of Ignatius is most easily explained by a residence of John in Asia and his natural death there. If John lived in Asia and died there a natural death, Ignatius could not have introduced his name into the letters as he introduced the names of Paul and Peter, for he wrote of both as martyrs (Rom. 4:3; Eph. 12:2). Aside from Paul and Peter, he named only living Christians. Peter and Paul were not named in any one of the remaining five of his letters. This might appear to indicate that, if we did not have his letters to the Romans and to the Ephesians, we should be justified in concluding that he did not know Peter and Paul had been in Rome; but the mere statement of such a conclusion shows how untrustworthy it would be. Even great men are not mentioned on all occasions and in every letter. Ignatius did not mention John because the nature of the letters he was writing was not such as to lead to such a mention.

In a similar way Polycarp's mention of Paul in his letter to the Philippians without a mention of John is readily accounted for. In one case (9.1, 2), he, like Ignatius, spoke of Paul as a martyr. In the other two references (3:2 and 11.2, 3) Paul's letter to the Philippians was the occasion of the mention. If, then, John lived in Asia for a time, died a natural death, and did not write a letter to the Philippians, Polycarp could not have mentioned John as he mentioned Paul. We can hardly assume that a letter from Polycarp to the Philippians must have mentioned John in any case. The lack of mention in the letter we have is accounted for if we assume that John did not die a martyr and did not write to the Philippians.

Papias' statement preserved by Eusebius (*H. E.* 3.39.3, 4) probably corroborates the theory that there was only one celebrated John in Asia and that this John was the son of Zebedee. This often-discussed statement includes the name John twice, but in each case it is applied to a presbyter. Eusebius, in his unfortunate guess concerning the authorship of the Apocalypse, had to interpret Papias' language to mean that Papias knew two Johns and located both of these in Asia. Papias certainly did not say this, and his language does not require such an interpretation. In the fact that the name John is each time given to a presbyter, together with the form of the verbs, is to be found the key to the language. The significant words are as follows: Εἰ δέ που καὶ παρηκολουθηκώς τις τοῖς πρεσβυτέροις ἔλθοι, τοὺς τῶν πρεσβυτέρων ἀνέκρινον λόγους· τί Ἀνδρέας .... εἶπεν .... ἢ τί Ἰωάννης .... ἅ τε Ἀριστίων καὶ ὁ πρεσβύτερος Ἰωάννης .... λέγουσιν. A comparatively simple interpretation of the somewhat ambiguous language is this: At the time of which Papias was writing —i. e., near the close of the first century—Andrew and the other presbyters named in the first part of the sentence, except John, were dead, and their younger associates, who told Papias of what they had said, spoke of each one in the past tense (εἶπεν).

Jesus' life and teachings, as he had heard them from John and others who had associated with Jesus. It is of great importance, therefore, to determine what these writings were in harmony with which Polycarp used to speak of Jesus' deeds and words. For this determination we must be guided by a consideration of the different possible meanings which ταῖς γραφαῖς may have in such a connection as that in which the expression here occurs.

The presence of the article without any other limitation of the noun indicates either that these were writings already mentioned in the preceding context, to which the article restricts them, or that they were the well-known writings which required no further description. As no writings are mentioned in the preceding context, we are limited to a consideration of the possible well-known writings. These appear to be the following:

1. The writings referred to were the well-known Old Testament Scriptures. This is possible, no doubt, for Irenaeus often interpreted the Old Testament statements as predictions of the events in Jesus' life. The context, however, has in it nothing to indicate that such a reference was intended here; rather, it seems to assure us that Irenaeus' interest here

---

Aristion and John were still alive, and the men who reported their teachings used the present tense (λέγουσιν). These two men were put in a different class, through a change in the form of the last part of the statement, because they were still alive at the time referred to. Aristion seems not to have been thought of as a presbyter; at any rate, he was not called one. But, in the case of John, the significantly restrictive ὁ πρεσβύτερος was used, apparently referring back to the fact that John had already been called a presbyter and intending to indicate directly that this John was the same one who had been mentioned in the first group and could now be mentioned again because he belonged also in the same class as Aristion.

The course of events, accordingly, was somewhat as follows: Papias, in his early life, used to inquire what the personal disciples of Jesus, while several of them were still alive, used to say. He inquired also what those still alive in his own time were saying. John, in view of the advanced age to which he attained, belonged to both classes. Papias, when he wrote in later life, preserved this distinction and repeated the descriptive phrase applied to John to show that it was the same man who was mentioned twice. His testimony is a testimony to one John, then, rather than to two. Where this one lived, either in the earlier period or the later, however, he did not say, for he did not locate any of the persons whom he named. Apparently the list is made without reference to location. Probably it was made for other reasons alone, namely, their relation to Jesus, as the language indicates. It is left to us, therefore, to locate John by means of evidence which we have from other sources than Papias. This will naturally lead us to say that, if Papias spoke of only one John and knew of him as one who had come to advanced age, the John whom he thus knew will almost certainly be the son of Zebedee, whom the testimony of Polycarp locates in Asia at the time of which Papias was speaking.

was in the accounts which he had of New Testament times—that he was appealing to history rather than to prophecy.

2. The writings referred to were the well-known New Testament writings as a whole. This, too, appears possible, for, in the days of Irenaeus, the New Testament had come to be referred to in that manner.[1] Such a reference, however, seems in no degree probable, for the New Testament as a whole does not describe the life and teachings of Jesus. If Irenaeus intended to refer to the New Testament at all, he could hardly have had in mind more of it than the gospels. We may pass, therefore, to consider the possibility of such a reference, namely,

3. Irenaeus referred to the well-known gospels of his own day. This may be resolved into three possibilities:

a. The four gospels existed in the time of Polycarp as they did in the time of Irenaeus. Irenaeus knew this and carelessly referred to them at the time of Polycarp by the title which they did not receive till a generation or two later. This theory has the serious difficulty that it must explain how the fourth gospel could have existed in the days of Polycarp and yet have no satisfactory attestation before about the year 170. Various explanations of this phenomenon have been attempted, but, up to the present time, no satisfactory solution of the difficulty seems to have been offered.

b) Irenaeus thought the four gospels existed in the time of Polycarp and carelessly described them by the title of his own time. He was right as to the existence of the synoptic gospels, but he was wrong concerning the fourth gospel, which, if it existed at all in Polycarp's day, did not exist in its present form. This theory differs from the preceding in that (1) it charges Irenaeus with a mistake concerning the date of the publication of the fourth gospel as well as concerning the title which he gave the gospels as they were known in Polycarp's day; (2) it assumes that the fourth gospel was not published till after the time of Polycarp, and so it does not need to explain the late attestation; (3) it has to explain how a "Johannine" gospel could have been published so late. Hitherto, attempts to explain how a "Johannine" gospel could have only such late attestation have either failed to give a satisfactory account of all the data involved, especially, per-

---

[1] Not so in the days of Polycarp. There is no instance in the works of the Apostolic Fathers which have come down to us where the gospels, or any part of the New Testament, or all of it together, is referred to as "the writings." The nearest approach to such an expression is in II *Clem.* 2.4, where, after passages from the Old Testament had been quoted, the writer continued: ἑτέρα δὲ γραφὴ λέγει, with a quotation of part of Matt. 9:13. Indeed, this is the only place in the Fathers where the gospel is referred to as γραφή.

haps, the practical absence of quotations by Justin from the fourth gospel,[1] or have largely discredited the idea that the fourth gospel was any very direct production of the son of Zebedee.

c) Irenaeus knew that the first three gospels were current in Polycarp's time as in his own; he knew also that the fourth gospel was a later work. In referring to the situation in the time of Polycarp, he merely employed the usage of his own time, not taking the trouble to state all the facts as he knew them. This theory relieves Irenaeus from responsibility for giving an early date to the publication of the fourth gospel, but it makes him responsible for error in carrying the title of the gospels in his own time back to the time of Polycarp. It, like the preceding, must give an explanation of the late appearance of a "Johannine" gospel.

Altogether, we cannot say certainly that the reference of Irenaeus was not to the well-known gospels of his own day. If the four gospels were in existence in the days of Polycarp, it would have been no very serious error, perhaps, for him to use the language which we are here considering. But, if we say that he merely employed the language of his own time, we become involved in one of two serious difficulties: either, (1) we must explain how the fourth gospel could have been current in the days of Polycarp, but failed to get any satisfactory attestation till considerably later, or, (2) we must show how a "Johannine" gospel could appear after Polycarp's time. In view of the recognized seriousness of these difficulties, especially the difficulty of securing any common ground between the two positions, it is worth while to consider a further possibility, namely,

4. Irenaeus referred to Johannine writings current and well-known in the days of Polycarp dealing with the work and teachings of Jesus, writings from which the fourth gospel was later compiled. There is no doubt that this is a real possibility. To be sure, we do not know that such Johannine writings existed; if we did, some of the most serious aspects of the Johannine problem would be removed. The expression which Irenaeus here used, however, may indicate that there were such writings. At any rate, the expression suggests a possibility; we may take it and see what it is worth. The following points are worthy of notice:

a) If there were such Johannine writings current and well known in the days of Polycarp, then the expression which Irenaeus used was a natural one with which to refer to them; his language is as natural for such writings in the time of Polycarp as the same language had come to be for a reference to the New Testament in his own day.

---

[1] Such references by Justin as that in *Apology* i. 61, for example, are sufficiently explained if Justin had Johannine material but not the fourth gospel.

b) This hypothesis relieves Irenaeus of the charge of carelessness and inaccuracy in making reference to the writings which he here had in mind. This is a comparatively unimportant matter, to be sure, but still it is worth taking into account. We have no occasion to discredit the man more than is necessary. The presumption ought to be that he is correct, until he is shown to be wrong, and a theory which justifies him in his usage is preferable, if it meets other conditions equally well.

c) This hypothesis is in accord with what appears to be the more obvious meaning of Irenaeus' language, for he seems to say that Polycarp used to speak in harmony with writings then in existence which were then known as "the" writings; if anyone reads the language without any prepossessions as to what writings are referred to, he will probably reach this conclusion.

d) If we look at the context, that appears to indicate that Irenaeus had in mind Johannine writings, but not a single gospel nor a gospel together with our Johannine epistles. The preceding context tells of the oral accounts which Polycarp used to give concerning Jesus as Polycarp had received them from John. The contents of these oral accounts are indicated by only two specific terms. These are αἱ δυνάμεις and ἡ διδασκαλία. Perhaps no other two terms alone could have been employed which would so well describe the special characteristics of the contents of the fourth gospel as distinguished from the contents of the synoptic accounts. The point is not decisive, to be sure, but it offers an interesting suggestion. It suggests that John used to speak especially of Jesus' miracles and teaching, that Polycarp used to repeat those accounts, and that the terms which Irenaeus selected to describe those accounts—because these terms best find their contents in our fourth gospel at the same time that Irenaeus spoke of "the writings" instead of "the gospel"—are testimony from the time of Polycarp to the contents of the fourth gospel as material which came from the son of Zebedee at the same time that Irenaeus' selection of "the writings," as a term to describe the written form of that material, is a testimony to Johannine writings as embodying that material. By supposing that there were Johannine accounts of Jesus' work and teaching—but not our fourth gospel—current in the time of Polycarp, we explain the language of Irenaeus' letters, both as to his selection of the term "the writings" and the context which indicates the contents of that term.

e) If we suppose that, in the time of Polycarp, there were Johannine writings, rather than a Johannine gospel, we gain an effective key to the problem of the long-recognized "displacements" in our fourth gospel. This recognition of displacements implies that, at some time, and in one form or another, our gospel existed in the shape of "booklets," as Professor Burton has happily named them. These booklets were produced, we may assume, no doubt, with no thought that they would ever form a single work; if the author, or authors, of them had intended a single work, he, or they, would not have made booklets. Such booklets very naturally included similar material, or even the same material, presented from different points of view, or even from apparently different situations. Their compilation into a whole—after the usual method of writing history of the time—would then result in just such apparent dislocations and inconsistencies as the critical reader may now find in the fourth gospel.[1] But if we suppose that the gospel was composed as a single work, even from sources, these apparent dislocations and inconsistencies can hardly be explained as anything less than carelessness or ignorance. The supposition, accordingly, that the Johannine story of the life and teachings of Jesus in the time of Polycarp, at least as far as it was written at that time, was in the form of separate booklets, enables us most easily and most satisfactorily to account for an important element of the internal evidence of the fourth gospel. The course of events leading up to its compilation, then, will have been somewhat as follows: John did not write a gospel as a single work. If he himself wrote of Jesus at all, his writings were only in the form of short disconnected accounts. Perhaps it is more probable that the writing was done by one of his disciples with his approval. Such accounts, short sermons as it were, dealing with different aspects of Jesus' life and teachings but incidentally overlapping one another, received recognition at once, but were not thought of as a gospel. They remained in use, in Asia Minor, at least, during the time of Polycarp, and were the Johannine writings in accord with which Polycarp used to speak of the miracles and teachings of Jesus. Polycarp recognized the writings, but he was not dependent upon them, for he had received the same accounts from John himself and could relate them independently. Some time after this, perhaps about the middle of the second century, such Johannine writings then current as would best serve the purpose were compiled into a gospel, and the compilation resulted in the internal characteristics which have led scholars to recognize either displacements or booklets in our fourth gospel.

f) If the Johannine writings in the time of Polycarp were merely booklets, we can readily understand Justin's failure to quote from the fourth gospel—there was no such gospel until about the time he wrote. If he knew of Johannine booklets, he did not honor them as he did the synoptic

---

[1] E. g., those found by Bacon as described in *The American Journal of Theology*, Vol. IV, under the title "Tatian's Rearrangement of the Fourth Gospel."

"memoirs." The increase in his use of Johannine material in the *Dialogue* as compared with that in the *Apology* (or the *Apologies*, if we call them two) is doubtless due largely to the increase in value for him of the Johannine material during the several years between the composition of the two works.

g) This view is not necessarily out of harmony with what Irenaeus himself wrote of the authorship of the gospel. His definite statement is as follows (3.1.1): Ἔπειτα Ἰωάννης ὁ μαθητὴς τοῦ Κυρίου, ὁ καὶ ἐπὶ τὸ στῆθος αὐτοῦ ἀναπεσών, καὶ αὐτὸς ἐξέδωκε τὸ εὐαγγέλιον, ἐν Ἐφέσῳ τῆς Ἀσίας διατρίβων. The καὶ αὐτός, as an emphatic repetition of Ἰωάννης, κτλ., plus the article with εὐαγγέλιον show that Irenaeus understood the work of the evangelist to have been merely to give his individual form to the common gospel story. This is usually understood to mean that Irenaeus made John the immediate author of the fourth gospel in the form in which Irenaeus had it. But the statement itself may mean much less than that. If it is compared with the immediately preceding statements concerning the authorship of the other gospels, one will see that Irenaeus seems to have made each of the other evangelists a writer of a completed gospel (Matthew γραφὴν ἐξήνεγκεν εὐαγγελίου; Mark ἐγγράφως ἡμῖν παραδέδωκε; Luke τὸ . . . . εὐαγγέλιον ἐν βιβλίῳ κατέκετο), while John simply ἐξέδωκε τὸ εὐαγγέλιον. Was this Irenaeus' way of saying that John did not prepare a complete gospel but merely left gospel material? That may hardly be asserted, but it is certainly a possibility, and it is truly suggestive. Irenaeus' language is capable of that meaning, and such a meaning put upon it allows a theory of the origin of the gospel which will explain its late attestation, its Johannine character, and Irenaeus' substantial accuracy—three data which the evidence as a whole has required us to reconcile, if such a reconcilation may be fairly secured.

Two objections will doubtless be offered against this interpretation of Irenaeus' language. It will be said that I have freely charged him (p. 24) with a mistake concerning the authorship of the third gospel, while I now attempt to explain away the ordinarily accepted meaning of his accompanying statement concerning the fourth gospel. But the two cases are not at all parallel. Irenaeus' mistake concerning the third gospel has been recognized on grounds independent of Irenaeus, who was much farther removed from the writing of the third gospel than from the writing of the fourth, and is much more likely not to have had accurate information concerning the third. Moreover, in the case of the fourth gospel, difficulties concerning it which are recognized by scholars on grounds independent of Irenaeus are best explained by accepting his statement concerning it as an accurate one, the correct interpretation of which I have just indicated. It is entirely possible, therefore, that Irenaeus' concise statement concerning the fourth gospel is the outcome of direct knowledge of its origin. Considerations to be advanced later, as well as those already advanced, support this view of the questions at issue.

The other objection will be that Irenaeus often quoted the fourth gospel as the actual language of John, which he ought not to have done if he knew that John himself did not write the gospel or even booklets from which it was compiled. The natural reply is that, on the theory of the origin of the gospel which I have proposed, John was sufficiently responsible for the language of the gospel for Irenaeus to have felt entire freedom in quoting it as John's, at least for such purposes as he had in mind.

This discussion of ταῖς γραφαῖς may now be summed up as a whole. The term was recognized in the time of Irenaeus as a title for the gospels, and he may have applied it to the gospels in the time of Polycarp, assuming, correctly or incorrectly, that they did so exist. To say that he did this, however, involves us in serious difficulty concerning the fourth gospel, a difficulty which hitherto has not been satisfactorily met, namely, to explain either (1) how our fourth gospel could have existed in the days of Polycarp as it existed in the days of Irenaeus without getting any attestation till about the year 170, or (2) how a Johannine gospel could have appeared only after Polycarp's time, in which case its late attestation would be explained by its late appearance. In short, to interpret Irenaeus' reference to "the writings" as a reference to the gospels is linguistically possible, but such an interpretation leaves us in historical difficulties.

The expression is equally explicable linguistically, however, as a reference to Johannine writings current in Polycarp's day; if there were such writings, the expression is the natural one for Irenaeus to have used to describe them. By assuming that there were such writings, therefore, we are able to avoid the historical difficulties at the same time that we show due regard to linguistic usage. Especially, we find an explanation for the serious difficulty offered by the external evidence, namely, an explanation of a Johannine gospel with only late second-century attestation. At the same time, we find also a key to the problem of the internal evidence offered by the so-called displacements, a key which is at once simpler and far less arbitrary than any other, and one by means of which we avoid depreciating the work of either author or editor of the gospel. No single item of the evidence warrants the conclusion which has been reached, but the ready combination, on this theory, of all the elements of the evidence in such a manner as to seem to solve the problem which has been before us offers a strong probability that the conclusion is correct.[1]

This testimony from Polycarp warrants a still further statement concerning the Johannine writings as they were known in Asia in Polycarp's time. As the testimony led above (p. 30) to the conclusion that Polycarp and those who received their information from him knew of only one John of prominence in Asia at the close of the first century, so here it implies that Polycarp and the rest knew of only one author for the Johannine writings. The only Johannine writer of whom they knew was the son of Zebedee. The opinion that the Johannine writings came from him was a uniform one. The very absence of discussion of the question is doubtless one reason why we do not have any more data bearing on the question. If there had been a difference of view concerning the authorship of the Johannine writings, such, e. g., as there was concerning the observance of Easter, it is natural to suppose that we should have inherited some accounts of the differences, as we have in the case of the differences about Easter. The testimony of the second century knows no such difference of views, and the recognition of this fact is highly important.[2]

[1] It may seem that, in this interpretation of ταῖς γραφαῖς, Irenaeus has been credited with an accuracy in the use of language out of harmony with the looseness which has been attributed to him earlier in the discussion (pp. 13, 18, 20, 22). But such an objection probably misses the real significance of the expression. It is hardly one which would have been chosen with conscious carefulness. Rather, it is an ordinary Greek usage, under such conditions as this letter seems to involve. If Irenaeus had written with conscious effort to be accurate, he would probably have employed some fuller expression, which would have revealed his endeavor to avoid any uncertainty in his meaning. In his unconsciousness of such effort he embodied accuracy in simplicity—if the above interpretation is correct—because an ordinary phrase was the one to accomplish that.

[2] The statement of Epiphanius (51.3) that the Alogi attributed the fourth gospel to Cerinthus is not a serious matter. Irenaeus wrote two centuries earlier than Epiphanius and was one of Epiphanius' chief sources; but he did not know anything of this Alogi claim. Instead, he understood (3.11.1) that the fourth gospel was written against Cerinthus (which might be true of booklets as well as of a complete gospel, of course). Epiphanius did not find in Irenaeus anything concerning the Cerinthian authorship of the gospel, and his statement certainly cannot weigh against that of Irenaeus. In addition to the fact that Epiphanius was so much later than Irenaeus, one has only to read his language to recognize that he was an intemperate and prejudiced writer and to discount his statement for that reason as well as for its lateness. Still further, and perhaps even more important, Epiphanius lumped the Alogi—i. e., those to whom he gave the name Alogi, for he says he coined the name—all together without regard to the chronological development of the movement which he had in mind. As far as his statement is concerned, the attributing of the fourth gospel to Cerinthus might have occurred only after the time of Irenaeus. That is doubtless the fact. The

This evaluation of the Irenaeus testimony concerning Polycarp, from which we discover that when Irenaeus spoke of Polycarp and his relations to John he was speaking on the basis of trustworthy information, brings us to a position where we can see the significance of two interesting passages in the *Heresies* which have often been stumbling-blocks in the way of the student of the fourth gospel.

One of these is the well-known passage at the close of 3.1.1, which has already been quoted (p. 37). Taken by itself, this may appear to be a statement without any sufficient historical knowledge, and the context does not give it any more definite support. But if it is read in the light of the above discussion of the relation between Irenaeus and Polycarp, it, like the statements of the two letters, may be regarded as substantially the testimony of Polycarp. What Irenaeus said concerning John in this case he received through Polycarp, just as he had received through Polycarp what he put into the letters.

Putting together the results up to this point, we shall see them to mean that the fourth gospel, though it came into existence some decades later than the synoptic gospels, had a history in some respects similar to theirs, at any rate similar to the history of the first and third. It came into existence as a compilation and passed through an editorial stage.

The second passage in the *Heresies* on which the above discussion of Irenaeus' relation to Polycarp throws light, is the statement in 3.11.1a, already referred to in another connection (p. 39, footnote 2), according to which Irenaeus understood that John wrote the fourth gospel "*auferre eum qui Cerintho insemininatus erat hominibus errorem, et multo prius ab his qui dicuntur Nicolaitae.*" If Irenaeus had no trustworthy knowledge concerning the origin of the gospel, then such a statement from him could be no more than a conjecture, an after-thought, a theory to account for the fact that in the prologue of the gospel he found material which served as excellent apologetic against the Cerinthians.

If, on the contrary, as the above discussion has endeavored to show, Irenaeus was not theorizing but was writing on the basis of trustworthy

---

untrustworthiness of his statement as representing a fact of the second century is made more certain in that Epiphanius himself says the Alogi claim was a pretense (προφασίζονται γὰρ οὗτοι αἰσχυνόμενοι ἀντιλέγειν τῷ ἁγίῳ Ἰωάννῃ). This implies a discussion of the matter. If such a discussion occurred as early as the time of Irenaeus, his statement in 3.11.1, without any reference to such a discussion, is a psychological impossibility, for he would not have let pass any such occasion to oppose those who attacked the views which he held. We are quite safe in saying that the Alogi claim, whatever there was in it, was of later date than Irenaeus and is of no value in comparison with what he gives us.

information; if Polycarp had said within his hearing, had told Florinus, had related to the Roman Christians, that John had spoken and written against Cerinthus, then we can readily understand why Irenaeus merely made the statement without any attempt to prove it. If Polycarp had related the same facts to others as well as to Irenaeus, Florinus, and the Roman Christians—as would have been most natural, if he used to tell the story at all—some of these would be younger than himself but older than Florinus and would easily have met with Irenaeus and recounted the facts. Now none of these hypotheses is impossible, or even improbable, and when their probability is taken into account, we discover the reason for the simplicity of Irenaeus' narrative. He was writing for his own generation, and it did not occur to him that things which were generally recognized needed any lengthy proof. He chose to employ himself in the discussion of matters over which there was division of opinion.[1]

Thus far this chapter has been an examination of the testimony from Irenaeus as contained in his statements concerning Polycarp. There remains an examination of what he wrote concerning the presbyters, for his relation to John and the fourth gospel hinges on what he knew through these as well as on what he knew through Polycarp. The relationship is not so apparent, perhaps, in the presbyter testimony as it is in that from

---

[1] This absence of statement on the part of Irenaeus concerning matters of which we should be glad to have his testimony at length is an aspect of his writings by means of which critics have often been led astray. They find Irenaeus arguing at length over the meaning of New Testament language (e. g., 2.22), and it is inferred that similar arguments ought to appear concerning the authorship of the New Testament writings. For example, it is urged that because Irenaeus did not say anything more about the authorship of the fourth gospel he did not know anything more about it. But to urge this is to overlook the fact that Irenaeus was writing an apology for his own times, not a New Testament introduction. It reveals a lack of appreciation of the conditions at the time when Irenaeus wrote. Because Irenaeus wrote without citing his authorities and proving that they were trustworthy, he appears often to have written without authority. But when his relation to Polycarp and those of Polycarp's time is taken into account, one discovers that he had such first-hand authority as not to be aware that he needed to present it, especially in a work which was written for another purpose.

Sometimes the critic not only fails to recognize that Irenaeus was not concerned to discuss questions of authorship, but makes him concerned primarily in authorship. The discussion of Bacon in the first volume of *The Hibbert Journal* is a conspicuous example of this error. "Irenaeus, passionate advocate of the Johannine authorship" of the fourth gospel, is Bacon's language (p. 515). When, a little later (pp. 516, 517), he offers an explanation for his conclusion, he writes: "Irenaeus literally 'compasses heaven and earth' to find an argument against those who denied the apostolic authorship. Because there are four winds, four elements, four zones of the earth, four pillars of heaven, four cherubim sustaining the throne of God, the folly is manifest of 'those

Polycarp, but it is hardly less worthy of consideration because not so apparent. Through it we are able to reconstruct the historical situation in which Irenaeus lived more generally and on a larger scale than we can through that from Polycarp. Accordingly, even though some of the discussion may appear to be remote from John and the fourth gospel, such is not really the case, and its apparent remoteness must not prejudge the examination.

This presbyter testimony is contained in twenty-three references which Irenaeus made to unnamed authorities, as follows (a more complete list of these references than has heretofore been given, I believe): 1. pref. 2a; 1.13.3c; 1.15.6; 2.22.5c; 3.17.4c; 3.23.3a; 4.p.2b; 4.4.2b; 4.27.1a; 4.27.1c; 4.27.2c; 4.28.1b; 4.30.1a; 4.31.1a; 4.32.1a; 4.41.2a; 5.5.1c; 5.17.4c; 5.30.1a; 5.33.3b; 5.36.1c; 5.36.2b; Eus. *H. E.* 5.20. A discussion of the meaning of each of these references would require a larger amount of space than may well be given to it in this essay. Indeed, such a discussion is unnecessary, for the studies of Lightfoot (*Biblical Essays*, pp. 45 ff.), Harnack (*Chron.* I, pp. 333 ff.), and Zahn (*Forschungen*, VI, pp. 53 ff.) have already covered much of the ground with thoroughness. I shall merely state their respective conclusions, therefore, that their positions may be understood, and shall then deal only with what appear to be

---

wretched men who wish to set aside that aspect presented by John's gospel.'" The reference is to *Heresies* 3.11.4–9. The reader will observe, even from the summary of Bacon—which is none too just toward Irenaeus' own language—that Irenaeus was insisting that the gospels were four in number, but was not discussing the question of gospel authorship. Even in the case of the fourth gospel, it was the things presented by the gospel which Irenaeus' opponents were setting aside, not its Johannine authorship. The question of authorship is not mentioned. If the reader will examine the extended discussion of Irenaeus itself he will probably conclude that the absence of a discussion of authorship is more marked than my brief statement has made it. He will observe that Bacon has mistaken general apologetic for a discussion of authorship.

The important work of Drummond (*An Inquiry into the Character and Authorship of the Fourth Gospel*, 1904) fails to do justice to Irenaeus, but in another way. In summing up the results of a study of the letter to Florinus, Drummond finds only that Irenaeus "professes to have the most distinct recollection" of the discourses of Polycarp (p. 208), and that "one thing appears to be quite certain, that there was some John in Asia Minor who was highly distinguished, and to whom Polycarp was in the habit of appealing as an authority of the first class, one who, if not an apostle, was to be ranked with apostles" (p. 209). In this conclusion, Principal Drummond has failed to do justice to Irenaeus by failing to bring out the worth of Irenaeus' testimony concerning the Asian John. The conclusion leaves us in uncertainty as to what Irenaeus meant and admits that the Asian John may have been some other than the son of Zebedee, when a more searching examination of the testimony gives us the son of Zebedee alone.

pivotal portions of the testimony, especially those portions which these scholars seem to have failed to do justice to.

Lightfoot did not discuss all the twenty-three references. Among those to which he gave attention he found five classes as follows: (1) A written source, represented by the references of 1.p.2a; 1.13.3c; 3.17.4c; and 1.15.6; (2) a probably unwritten source, represented by 4.27.1a ff.; (3) an apparently written source, represented by 3.23.3a; (4) a probably written source, represented by 4.41.2a; (5) a written source, represented by 5.5.1c, and 5.36.1c and 2b. Of these the second, fourth, and fifth "present more or less distinct coincidences with St. John's Gospel" (p. 61). The fifth class he regarded as a written source because "Irenaeus uses the present tense 'the elders *say*,' and yet the persons referred to belonged to a past generation and were no longer living when he wrote" (p. 62). Lightfoot thought it probable that the fourth and the fifth classes might be united into one, both being thus found to be references to the work of Papias. His conclusion is significant for the following discussion in three ways:

1. It recognizes that some of these references which Irenaeus made to his unnamed authorities have no bearing on the fourth gospel.

2. It finds that some of the references which have a bearing on the fourth gospel are to oral sources.

3. It accepts the remainder of the references as made to a written source.

The conclusion of Lightfoot is shared by Harnack to the extent that he recognizes the three points just made. He disagrees with Lightfoot in that he divides the references as a whole into three classes only and reaches a different conclusion as to those which have a bearing on the fourth gospel.

Zahn differs from both Lightfoot and Harnack by finding only two classes among the references as a whole—those which have no bearing on the fourth gospel, and those which do have a bearing, all these latter being references to oral tradition.

Of these three discussions and conclusions, those of Harnack and Zahn are certainly the more important. Lightfoot, if he were still living and studying the Irenaeus testimony, would undoubtedly revise his statements in view of the studies which have appeared since his time. I shall assume, therefore, that his discussion is superseded and shall confine myself to the points in which Harnack and Zahn agree, and those in which they differ, as a means of discovering where their investigations are to be supplemented.

Harnack and Zahn agree that the following references have no particular bearing on the questions raised by the fourth gospel: 1.p.2a; 1.13.3c; 1.15.6; 3.17.4c, 3.23.3a; 4.p.2b; 4.4.2b; 4.41.2a; 5.17.4c. These references are so uncertain that we cannot be sure to what sources Irenaeus here referred. Perhaps he referred to several different persons. At any rate, none of the material which he attributed to the persons he so obscurely referred to appears to throw light on the fourth gospel.

Having thus eliminated nine of the twenty-three references first enumerated, the chief question in the study of the remaining fourteen is: Did Irenaeus here make use of oral sources, or of written ones? On this question Harnack and Zahn again agree in making the seven citations of 4.27.1a; 4.27.1c; 4.27.2c; 4.28.1b; 4.30.1a; 4.31.1a; and 4.32.1a refer to an oral source. Their agreement gives strong probability that the conclusion is correct. My own study of the passages leads to the same result.

The great gulf between the conclusion of Harnack and that of Zahn is the result of the different interpretations which they make of six out of the seven remaining passages, namely, 2.22.5c; 5.5.1c; 5.30.1a; 5.33.3b; 5.36.1c, and 5.36.2b. Zahn concludes that the reference in each of these six instances is to an oral source, and that all of them belong to the same class as the seven which have just been considered. Harnack concludes that these six references are to a written source, which he takes to be the work of Papias. These six references must be thoroughly examined, therefore, in order to discover, if possible, whether Harnack or Zahn is correct as to the form of the source which Irenaeus here used.

Before proceeding to that examination, however, it is desirable to notice that the remaining one of the twenty-three references (Eus. *H. E.* 5.20; the letter to Florinus) also properly belongs to the material to be examined, though both Harnack and Zahn have practically left it out of account in evaluating the presbyter testimony.[1] It must be considered in the evaluation because it not only contains a reference to the presbyters but also, at the same time, gives us testimony concerning Polycarp, thus furnishing a point of contact between the Irenaeus testimony which has already been examined and that which is now before us. Accordingly, we have

---

[1] Harnack considered the letter to some extent in his discussion of Polycarp, but only incidentally and meagerly in his discussion of the presbyters, not as having any important bearing on the question of the significance of the presbyter testimony.

Zahn enumerates (p. 60) "die wirklich hieher gehörigen Stellen, an welchen die citirten Gewährsmänner entweder geradezu oder vermöge des Zusammenhangs mit anderen Anführungen als Apostelschüler charakterisirt sind," but no part of the letter to Florinus appears in the list. He, like Harnack, appears to have regarded the letter as of prime significance only for the discussion of Polycarp.

My evaluation of the presbyter testimony, on the contrary, will be found to hinge largely on the element of it which is found in the letter to Florinus.

seven passages (2.22:5c; 5.5.1c; 5.30.1a; 5.33.3b; 5.36.1c; 5.36.2b, and Eus. *H. E.* 5.20) as those which are pivotal for the study to discover whether Irenaeus, in them, referred to a written source or to an oral one.

In 2.22.5 Irenaeus was discussing Jesus' age. With his method, the validity of his argument, or the results at which he arrived, we are not concerned. We desire merely to discover what there is in his reference to indicate the kind of source which he was employing. He wrote that "*a quadragesimo et quinquagesimo anno declinat* [a man] *iam in aetatem seniorem, quam habens Dominus noster docebat, sicut evangelium* καὶ πάντες οἱ πρεσβύτεροι μαρτυροῦσιν, οἱ κατὰ τὴν 'Ασίαν 'Ιωάννῃ τῷ τοῦ Κυρίου μαθητῇ συμβεβληκότες, παραδεδωκέναι ταῦτα τὸν 'Ιωάννην. . . . *Quidam autem eorum non solum Ioannem, sed et alios apostolos viderunt, et haec eadem ab ipsis audierunt et testantur de huiusmodi relatione.*" The question is: Did Irenaeus here make the presbyters a written source, or an oral one? The question must be answered from the material offered by the quotation, for there is nothing more in the context which gives evidence of coming from the source quoted.

In favor of the source being written, it will be noticed that Irenaeus appealed to the gospel in the same way in which he appealed to the presbyters. The gospel is the written gospel, for, in the context, quotation is made from both Luke and John. Beside the written gospel are juxtaposed the words, "the presbyters." At first thought such a juxtaposition appears to make the form of the source in the case of the presbyters the same as in the case of the gospel; as the gospel source was written, so also the presbyter source was written. Further consideration of the statement, however, shows that this conclusion does not take all the data into account and is not inevitable. A loose writer like Irenaeus might make such a juxtaposition incidentally rather than significantly. That the two substantives are thus united into a single general predicate—μαρτυροῦσιν can hardly be called more precise than that—indicates such looseness of expression as to weaken the argument from juxtaposition, unless juxtaposition is regarded in itself as decisive.

In favor of the source being oral is the fact that it is plural, "the presbyters." To be sure, even two or more presbyters might have united in the composition of a work in which they discussed Jesus' age as a teacher. But such a thing is not at all probable. If it had been done, some better indication of the fact than anything we have here would be likely to have shown itself. Harnack thinks their discussion had been embodied in written form by Papias but continued to be referred to as the work of the presbyters. This, too, is possible, but his conclusion is not convincing on the basis of this passage alone. The verb used—μαρτυροῦσιν was evidently the verb in both sentences of the Greek which Irenaeus wrote—perhaps points toward the conclusion that the source was oral, but, in the usage of Irenaeus, it cannot be regarded as decisive.

Altogether, though the passage is an important one, it does not furnish sufficient evidence to determine whether its source was written or oral. Whether the source was written or oral must be left an open question until the evidence of the other similar passages is taken into account.

When we pass to 5.5.1c, we do not find anything more definite. The language is not sufficiently different to warrant the space of quotation. Still more unfortunately, neither one of the closely associated references of 5.30.1a; 5.33.3b; 5.36.1c, or 5.36.2b adds anything of significance to that which is given in 2.22.5c. Some of them give more of the contents of the source from which Irenaeus drew, but these contents are not material which can determine the form of the source which he used. The separate discussion of each reference would be largely repetition. There is the less occasion for such discussion because both Harnack and Zahn regard all of these five references as belonging to the same class as 2.22.5c, Harnack putting them all together as written, Zahn making them all oral. Undoubtedly they will continue to be classed together, but whether the class will be made written or oral will depend, I believe, on evidence yet to be considered.

The letter to Florinus offers that more significant language. It has already been quoted (p. 26), but the portions bearing especially on the source of the presbyter testimony may appropriately be repeated. They are as follows: Ταῦτα τὰ δόγματα οἱ πρὸ ἡμῶν πρεσβύτεροι, οἱ καὶ τοῖς ἀποστόλοις συμφοιτήσαντες, οὐ παρέδωκάν σοι. Εἶδον γάρ σε . . . . ἐν τῇ κάτω Ἀσίᾳ παρὰ τῷ Πολυκάρπῳ . . . . διαμνημονεύω . . . . τὴν μετὰ Ἰωάννου συναναστροφὴν ὡς [Πολύκαρπος] ἀπήγγελλε. . . . .

A comparison of this language with that of 2.22.5c (see p. 45) will show at once the similarities between the two narratives. Attention may be called to some of the more important of these similarities: The presbyters are mentioned in the letter just as they were in the other passage; here, as there, they are men who had seen the apostles and associated with them;[1] the teaching which these presbyters handed down was, in both cases, that which they had received from John; the common place of activity was Asia.

The obvious conclusion from the discovery of such close similarities

[1] For determining who the apostles here referred to were, the reader should recall here, as elsewhere, the discussion of Irenaeus' use of the word "apostle" early in this essay (pp. 20–23).

between the two passages is, that the presbyters in the one case are of the same class as the presbyters in the other, and that the teaching on the basis of which Irenaeus made his appeal to Florinus is out of the same treasury as that on the basis of which he made appeal to those who should read the *Heresies*. If in the *Heresies* narrative Irenaeus employed a written source, then quite certainly the source which he used in the letter to Florinus was written. But if the former was oral, the latter likewise was doubtless oral.[1] The similarities between the two passages appear all the more striking when it is noted that the letter to Florinus was probably written some years after the passage in the *Heresies* and, naturally, without any thought that the two would ever be compared.

The conclusion thus reached involves a similar conclusion for the references of 5.5.1c; 5.30.1a; 5.33.3b; 5.36.1c, and 5.36.2b, since these references have already (p. 46) been assigned to the same class as 2.22.5c. The seven references together will be found to be alike, either written or oral, as far as the evidence already considered can indicate.

But there is an interesting difference between the language of the letter to Florinus and the language of 2.22.5c. In 2.22.5c the verb which Irenaeus used to describe the presbyter source is in the present tense ($\mu\alpha\rho\tau\upsilon\rho\circ\hat{\upsilon}\sigma\iota\nu$), while in the letter to Florinus the verb is in the past tense ($\pi\alpha\rho\acute{\epsilon}\delta\omega\kappa\alpha\nu$). This difference appears the more significant when one observes that the verbs of 5.5.1c; 5.30.1a; 5.33.3b; 5.36.1c, and 5.36.2b, are all presents. The difference is made more suggestive when we recognize that the verbs of 4.27.1a; 4.27.1c; 4.27.2c; 4.28.1b; 4.30.1a; 4.31.1a, and 4.32.1a are all in the past tense. The past tense appears natural for a reference to oral testimony of men who were no longer living, apparently, at the time when Irenaeus wrote, but to use the present tense for such a reference seems to require explanation. The need of explanation appears to be increased when we take into account that the presbyter of 4.27.1a; 4.27.1c; 4.27.2c, and perhaps the presbyters of 4.28.1b to 4.32.1a, were one generation farther from the apostles than Polycarp;[2] for, though

[1] Harnack has led astray the readers of his interpretation of the letter to Florinus by making significant Irenaeus' choice of σοι at the close of the first sentence quoted above. He thinks that the choice of σοι instead of ἡμῖν indicates that Irenaeus himself could not look back to such a relationship with the presbyters as Florinus could. His inference certainly appears forced, for it is a strange conception of a letter according to which σοι, chosen evidently to emphasize the fact that the recipient of the letter knew certain things, excluded μοι on the part of the writer, especially when the writer proceeds directly to speak of these same things as those which he himself recalled.

[2] Irenaeus' descriptive phrase in 4.27.1a is: "*Audivi a quodam presbytero, qui audierat ab his qui apostolos viderant.*"

these men seem to have been farther from the apostles, and therefore nearer to Irenaeus, the verbs which refer to their testimony are put in the past tense, while the verbs referring to the testimony of those who were nearer the apostles are put in the present tense. Is this an indication that Harnack —though he did not discuss this element of the testimony—was correct in concluding that 2.22.5c, etc., imply a written source?

Before an answer is given, two other data offered by the letter to Florinus must be considered. First, in this letter Polycarp is one of the presbyters, for the teachings to which Irenaeus was exhorting Florinus to return were teachings which Florinus had received from Polycarp as one of the presbyters. This is certainly the meaning of the later portion of the letter (see p. 26), where Irenaeus reminded Florinus specifically of the teaching of Polycarp and of the fact that this teaching had come from John and others who had seen the Lord. The connective γάρ after εἶδον also shows that the statement which it introduces relating to Polycarp is explanatory of the preceding statement concerning the presbyters, one of whom, therefore, Polycarp must have been considered. This conclusion is made certain a little later when Polycarp is expressly called a presbyter.

The second datum to be taken into account is, that the testimony from Polycarp in this letter to Florinus—and so the testimony of all of these presbyters, in view of the conclusion of the above paragraph—is plainly oral. We are sure of this because Irenaeus insisted that he was recalling from memory the teachings to which he urged Florinus' attention. His language implies clearly that Florinus, likewise, had received the instruction in question orally. The oral nature of this testimony from Polycarp and the other presbyters is further brought out by Irenaeus' language at the close of the letter. After he had spoken of Polycarp and his teaching as Florinus and himself had received information orally, he continued: Καὶ ἐκ τῶν ἐπιστολῶν δὲ αὐτοῦ . . . . δύναται φανερωθῆναι. The oral testimony which Florinus had received might be corroborated by written statements to the same effect in the letters of Polycarp still current at the time when Irenaeus wrote.

The evidence seems, therefore, to point in two directions. The verbs in the present tense in the references to the presbyter testimony of 2.22.5, etc., favor the conclusion that this testimony was from a written source. On the other hand, the striking similarities between the contents of the testimony of the letter—which has been found to be certainly oral—and the contents of the other testimony favor the conclusion that all of the presbyter testimony was oral. Can this apparent discrepancy be explained?

There seems to be no way of minimizing the significance of the common contents of the two statements of Irenaeus except to say that the similarities are mere chance and to deny them any determining weight. This would not be an explanation and would still leave unaccounted for the fact that the letter to Florinus contains presbyter testimony which is certainly oral, while the same kind of testimony in the *Heresies* is regarded as written. It is worth while, therefore, to inquire whether Irenaeus may have employed the verbs in the present tense to refer to an oral tradition handed down from an earlier time. Grammatical usage appears to warrant such an explanation in either of two ways. The verbs may be regarded as historical presents, in which case they are a vivid means of calling attention to the impressiveness of the testimony which the presbyters gave; or they may be regarded as progressive presents, in which case Irenaeus conceived of the testimony from the presbyters as so vital and permanent, through its repetition by men of his own time, that the presbyters were still speaking. The thought of Irenaeus is not essentially different by the adoption of one of these explanations from what it is by the adoption of the other. From which point of view he conceived them as he wrote, we can hardly conclude with certainty. I think it probable, however, that he regarded the presbyters as still speaking through the men of his own time, and that we should therefore describe the verbs as progressive presents.[1]

The argument thus presented for the oral form of the presbyter testimony which Irenaeus used is supplemented by a statement in the midst of the testimony which appears to exclude the conclusion that the testimony was written. This statement is a reference to the work of Papias at the beginning of 5.33.4, in which we read: Ταῦτα [referring back to testimony which had just been attributed to the presbyters] δὲ καὶ Παπίας Ἰωάννου μὲν ἀκουστής, Πολυκάρπου δὲ ἑταῖρος γεγονώς, ἀρχαῖος ἀνήρ, ἐγγράφως ἐπιμαρτυρεῖ ἐν τῇ τετάτῃ τῶν αὑτοῦ βίβλων. The καί, which is strengthened by

---

[1] It may still be asked why Irenaeus used the past tense so regularly in some instances (4.27.1a, etc.) and the present with equal regularity in other cases (2.22.5c, etc.). I offer the following explanation: If these citations are considered from the point of view of the composition of his work, they occur at four points. The passage in 2.22.5c stands by itself, the only one of the references which occurs in the second book. The seven references of 4.27.1a, etc., are evidently from one, or practically one, sitting of the writer. That of 5.5.1c, like 2.22.5c, occurs apart by itself. The last four references of the fifth book have a contiguity similar to the contiguity of the seven in the fourth book. At the first, third, and fourth of these points Irenaeus thought, and expressed himself, through historical, or progressive, presents. In the second, he thought, and expressed himself, through a past tense. Probably everyone who has observed himself or other writers has recognized these tense "moods." The phenomenon may be observed in printed books. It will doubtless be found in this essay, though I have consciously sought to avoid it.

the ἐπί in composition, shows that Irenaeus had material from Papias in addition to that which he derived from the presbyters. The ἐγγράφως shows that the material from Papias was written and implies that the material from the presbyters was oral. If Irenaeus had not desired to emphasize the written form of the material from Papias as over against the oral from the presbyters, his meaning was complete without the ἐγγράφως. The distance of ἐγγράφως from the καί likewise indicates that he was keeping such a distinction in mind.[1]

I conclude with Zahn, therefore, that Irenaeus, when he referred to the presbyters, was employing an oral tradition. The basis of my conclusion, however, is markedly different from Zahn's. He noted that the citations of 5.5.1c, etc., were referred by Irenaeus to "the presbyters," or to "the presbyters, disciples of the apostles," and, without more critical evaluation of the reference, concluded (p. 71): "Es ist also ohne Frage derselbe Kreis von Männern gemeint wie in den Citaten Nr. 1 und 2–8" (i. e., 2.22.5 and the seven in 4.27.1–4.32.1; for he had already concluded, p. 62, on the basis of a more extended discussion, but one no more convincing because largely irrelevant, that 2.22.5 belongs to the same class as the citations in book four). It is not surprising that Harnack has not been convinced by such treatment of important material. One wonders how Zahn

---

[1] The distinction between his sources which Irenaeus thus made is similar to the distinction which he made in the letter to Florinus (p. 48). In each case, the oral source was used first and then confirmed by a reference to a written source.

Harnack has strangely disregarded the ἐγγράφως in his discussion (p. 336), not even mentioning it; and this enabled him to use the δὲ καί not only to show that the Papias testimony was confirmatory, but also that it was of the same form as that of the presbyters. Harnack thinks it would be strange, if the testimony from the presbyters was oral, that Irenaeus should have found the same testimony in the written work of Papias. The objection appears convincing only if we assume a *verbatim* similarity between the two sources. But such an assumption is surely not necessary. If Irenaeus found in Papias' work a statement of substantially the same things as those which had come to him through the oral tradition of the presbyters, the requirements of his language are sufficiently met.

Bacon has obscured Irenaeus' distinction in a different way when he translates the phrase in question as follows (*The Hibbert Journal*, II, p. 330): "These things Papias, who was a hearer of John . . . . witnesses in writing in the fourth of his books." This translation is clearly a disregard of the significant connectives which Irenaeus used.

In 4.41.2a Irenaeus made a distinction between authorities which further illustrates his usage in such matters. In this passage, for the support of his interpretation of the word "*filius,*" he added: "*Quemadmodum et quidam ante nos dixit.*" The "*et*" shows the additional source, but no further words were used to indicate that the second source was of a different kind.

himself, especially after the appearance of Harnack's *Chronologie*, could expect that such treatment would suffice.

On the other hand, I have rejected the conclusion of Harnack that the presbyter testimony of 2.22.5c, etc., was written only after taking into account important data which he did not use and after subjecting all the data involved to a more searching and exhaustive examination than he has offered.

In some ways, at least, as already mentioned (p. 42), this extended examination of the testimony which Irenaeus attributed to the presbyters appears to be remote from the fourth gospel, perhaps even remote from the question of the significance of the Irenaeus testimony to the fourth gospel. It is, however, of very great importance, next in importance, in fact, to the testimony from Polycarp. Indeed, in the letter to Florinus, as we have seen, it is the testimony of Polycarp and, by virtue of this, connects the two classes of testimony closely together.

But it has a further value, also, in view of which its examination is particularly in place in this essay. By means of it we are able to discover, as we otherwise should hardly be able to do, the general situation in which Irenaeus lived, and the historical and intellectual atmosphere about him. We see from it how close Irenaeus felt himself to be to the days of the apostles, and, as we do this, we are in a position to understand his language, which, for those who demand specific statements from him as to the source of his information, is by no means as convincing as it might be, but, when his position is taken into account, is such language as might be expected. He wrote for the people of his own time. Even the *Heresies* was only a tract for the times, extended and verbose, to be sure, but written to meet existing need. In a work thus produced, explanations about his authorities and his relation to Asia, the means of communication which were employed, and the transmission of news would have been highly gratuitous. He and all his readers knew who the presbyters were, and he took their knowledge for granted.

It is a serious mistake, therefore, to think that Irenaeus, born in Asia and living there till he was at least a youth, should have maintained the interest in Asia and Asian affairs so manifest in his writings, and yet have been practically cut off from his native land. Some writers proceed as though Polycarp and Irenaeus were the only men of the second century and Irenaeus could not have known anything of Asia except what he received directly from Polycarp. It is forgotten that the removal of Irenaeus from Asia to Gaul, the removal of Florinus from Asia to Rome (cf. Eus. *H. E.* 5.20 with 5.15), and the visit of Polycarp to Rome are evidently only incidental examples of visits and changes which were occurring frequently, by means of which important information was the common property of Christians throughout the empire.

Indeed, for those who are ready to transport themselves back in thought into Irenaeus' time, to reconstruct the activities which were occurring about him, to think of his relation to Asia and of his natural communication with Asian friends, to recognize that there were men only a little younger than Polycarp who could scarcely have failed to be leavened with his thought or to transmit it to their younger companions, to think of how such men readily became the means for the distribution of the treasured apostolic information, to realize that the several letters of Polycarp still extant in Irenaeus' day (see p. 27) were only representative of the correspondence which carried information over the empire but retained it in the personal form rather than in one which would be called history, or narratives—for those who are willing to restore the life of the second century in such ways as these, only much more fully than this outline indicates, the testimony of the presbyters and its introduction without any explanation or naming of the individuals other than Polycarp, as well as the importance which it had for Irenaeus, are only the most natural phenomena. He who thus relives the times, who is not content simply to scrutinize the documents grudingly and accept only what they rigidly require, is merely an instance of the historian who not only goes back *to* the documents but back *of* the documents, a process without which no history is ever truly written.[1]

What has just been said should not be interpreted as a minimizing of documents. Too much has been made of them in this essay to warrant such an inference as that. It is intended only to insist that documents alone may be merely what the skeleton is to the body; we could not get along without the skeleton, but, if we decline to accept anything more than its various bones, we shall never know the body from which it came. Irenaeus' testimony is only a skeleton on which to restore a body. The presbyter portion shows where some of the outlines are to be filled in and indicates the form which the body will take when it is complete. We are poor historians if we cling to the bones only and refuse to make the restoration as the outlines are given to us.

[1] A modern instance of similar import is in point. Shall it be said that I do not know the substantial facts concerning Johann Oncken's baptism in the River Elbe in 1834, because I never knew him, nor Barnas Sears, nor heard the story of the baptism from anyone who heard it from either of them, nor, as far as I know, read of the baptism from the writings of anyone who knew Oncken or Sears, personally? Yet I am much more likely to be in error concerning that incident than Irenaeus was to be in error concerning the John of Asia.

The outcome of such a readiness to transfer oneself back into the second century and relive its conditions is a recognition that Irenaeus was in a position to know well the important facts of the situation in Asia at the close of the first century. He could know, as thoroughly as current and widespread opinion could give it to him, the Asian thought about the Asian John and any writings which he left. Though he may never have seen Polycarp except when he listened to him in his youth—and probably he did not—he would still be able to know of him and his work with fulness and accuracy through the accounts of men who had associated with Polycarp in his later years and afterward had met Irenaeus or had otherwise communicated with him. It is by no means improbable that Pothinus had occupied such a place. If he did not, others might easily and naturally have done so.

The failure of Irenaeus to mention the names of any of the presbyters except Polycarp is not strange when Irenaeus' custom in the use of names is taken into account. It seems to have been an idiosyncrasy of his not to make use of names. Perhaps few students have paused to consider that even Polycarp is mentioned in only one passage of the entire *Adversus Haereses* (3.3.4). Papias is named only once (5.33.4a). Ignatius is quoted once (5.28.4c), but his name is not mentioned. He was to Irenaeus simply "a certain man of ours." Shall we say in view of this that Irenaeus did not know his name? Probably we shall not. But, if he knew Ignatius and yet quoted him without naming him, is it strange that he did not name the presbyters, other than Polycarp, to whom he referred? He may have known the names of several of them and yet have chosen to omit their names, since, as he felt, at least, the addition of their names would not enhance the value of his work. Harnack's conclusion (p. 334) that because Irenaeus did not mention any more of the names of the presbyters he did not know any more must regretfully be regarded as a lack of appreciation of Irenaeus' personal bearing in the matter of names and of the usage which resulted from it.

The recognition that these presbyters were felt by Irenaeus to be so near to him and that the testimony which he had from them was oral explains how that testimony could be at once most highly regarded and least trustworthy. It was most highly regarded because it had all the freshness of apparent personality. It was least trustworthy because it had suffered the transformation of all oral tradition.

The story of Jesus' age (2.22.5) is an interesting example of this combination of high regard and untrustworthiness. If Irenaeus found that story in a written source which dated from the early part of the second century and had its origin in a sub-apostolic circle, no very creditable explanation of its origin is available. But, if he got the idea of Jesus' age from oral tradition, it is a comparatively easy matter to understand how tradition, in the course of more than three-quarters of a century, should have developed into the story which Irenaeus related. Its oral transmission and development accounts for its lack of harmony with the early written records, but the personal element in its oral form made it appear more important to Irenaeus than the statements of the gospels themselves. Accordingly, he used the oral tradition first to prove that Jesus lived to be forty or fifty years old, and then, by a forced interpretation of John 8:56, 57, he attempted to bring this, his secondary authority, into harmony with the oral testimony, which to him was of first importance.[1]

This use of the oral tradition side by side with the written gospels by Irenaeus presents what to us may be a strange fusion of authorities, but it was not such to him. He was absolutely sure there were only four gospels which were to be recognized (3.11.8), of which the gospel according to John was one; yet, by the side of this and of superior importance, if the

[1] There can be no doubt that Irenaeus did regard the oral authority of the presbyters as more direct and more important. This is shown by the form in which he introduced the gospel statement: "*Sed et ipsi .... Iudaei .... significaverunt*," in which the "*et*" shows that this statement is confirmatory of the preceding argument. Of course it is possible for a confirmatory statement to be regarded as equal in importance with the one which it confirms. The more important statement may even be reserved till the last as a climax. But I have no idea that anyone who reads this and other passages of Irenaeus will attribute such logical or rhetorical arrangement to him. He placed first that which was the important consideration. Afterward that which was less important was introduced to corroborate. The case here of the age of Jesus is similar to that in the argument to Florinus, where the oral tradition of the presbyters was placed first and then a reference made to the letters of Polycarp (p. 27), in which the same material could be found. A still further case is that of the presbyters and Papias already discussed (p. 51), where again the oral authority of the presbyters received the place of importance.

The recognition of the superiority of the oral presbyter testimony for Irenaeus is important because it enforces once more the certainty of Irenaeus' feeling of nearness to the apostles and their teaching and indicates again the way in which we are to understand Irenaeus when he wrote of apostolic tradition.

Through the medium of the presbyter tradition, we readily understand why John 14:2 was so loosely quoted in 5.36.2a. Irenaeus' own direct quotations were loose enough, as we have seen (p. 12); when he was only quoting from an oral transmission of Jesus' words, the freedom here is what we might expect. Whether the presbyters got this statement entirely from oral tradition or from one of the Johannine "booklets" is unimportant. The following sentence, "*Quemadmodum Verbum eius* [God] *ait: 'Omnibus divisum esse a Patre secundum quod quis est dignus, aut erit,'* " thus attributed to Jesus, not, however, found in our gospels, but doubtless, as Stieren thought, belonging "*ad dictum Christi, Irenaeo traditum a presbyteris veteribus, quos saepissime*

two did not agree, was the oral tradition from the presbyters, which came to him as personal testimony still fresh with its personal life and vividness. Such an insistence on four gospels as the only ones, at the same time that the oral tradition was valued even more highly, may appear to us to be an inconsistency, but it was not that to him. He did not even become aware that such a use of authorities required any explanation, and this probably means that such a view of gospel material was the common one in his day, at least one the appropriateness of which was not disputed. In fact, others were more liberal than he, for his insistence on only four gospels indicates that others would have accepted more than four. Gospel accounts, both written and oral, were evidently common possessions; the apostolic tradition, especially that from John of Asia, was familiar and fully recognized. When Irenaeus spoke of the writer of the fourth gospel as "the disciple of the Lord who also leaned upon his breast" (3.1.1c), he at once recalled for his readers the rich oral tradition which was current among the Christians of his day, and they filled in the outline. For this

laudat," may indicate that the presbyter form of this John passage was entirely oral. We may be quite certain, at any rate, that Irenaeus did not think of it, on the occasion of his writing this passage, as being a quotation from his Johannine gospel. Whether Irenaeus was thinking directly of the gospel when he wrote 3.19.3c, where the Latin has the same words as in 5.36.2a, it is impossible to determine, for there is no reference given to any authority. In the tables at the beginning of this essay, I have called 3.19.3c a "reference" to the gospel but have made 5.36.2a a "quotation," because of the different ways in which Irenaeus introduced the two allusions to the gospel. It is one of Irenaeus' uses of the gospel which illustrate the difficulty of making rules to describe the different kinds of reference which he employed.

The recognition of the superiority of the oral testimony for Irenaeus is highly important for the understanding of his statement in the recently discovered Armenian MS, according to which Irenaeus wrote (translation of Fred C. Conybeare, *The Expositor*, July, 1907, p. 43): "Now faith assigns (*or* guarantees) us this [salvation] just as the elders, the disciples of the apostles, handed (it) down. In the first place it prescribes remembrance of the fact that we have received baptism for the remission of sin into name of God the Father and into name of Jesus Christ, the Son of God made flesh and dead and risen, and into Holy Spirit of God." As soon as one recognizes that the tradition of the elders was primary for Irenaeus, he will not say, with Conybeare: "Why should Irenaeus, if he had before him the direct precept of the Lord to baptize in the name of Father, Son and Holy Spirit (Matt. 28:19), thus invoke the tradition of the elders? . . . . Moreover, the true formula as here given is quite unlike that of Matt. 28:19." He becomes aware that the formula which Irenaeus used is unlike that of Matthew just because Irenaeus was following the tradition of the presbyters, which, though degenerate, was the authority which he preferred. He had such a formula from tradition, naturally, because a formula for such a service as baptism would be one of those most likely to be transmitted orally, and to have developed in the Asian circle of Christians somewhat differently from that of the first gospel.

tradition Irenaeus himself was doubtless largely responsible, since he must often have told to the many Christians whom he had met in his varied ministries such details as those which are merely touched upon in the letter to Florinus, details for which he was under obligation to Polycarp and those who had associated with Polycarp, older than himself but younger than Polycarp. No doubt he had received much of this material from Florinus himself, who had been more closely associated with Polycarp and apparently had been Irenaeus' close friend for many years.

CONCLUSION

The Irenaeus testimony which has been examined is of two quite different kinds, but the examination has led to a single result. In the case of the testimony which Irenaeus derived from Polycarp, the study has been chiefly a critical investigation of the meaning of Irenaeus' language in the two important letters which have come down to us. That study has seemed to give good evidence for believing that the celebrated John of Asia was the son of Zebedee and that he was responsible for Johannine writings which were current during the first half of the second century. The study of the testimony which Irenaeus attributed to the presbyters has been equally critical, but it has given no direct information concerning John or the Johannine writings. It has shown, however, how near Irenaeus felt himself to be to the apostles of the first century. That feeling of nearness to the apostles was recognized, to be sure, in the letters to Victor and Florinus, but in the presbyter testimony it becomes much more prominent, though this greater prominence is seen not so much in express statement as in the unexpressed but conscious assurance of that nearness which his language implies. He felt himself so directly in contact with apostolic teaching, and so fully assumed the recognition of this on the part of his readers, that he did not think of explaining why he had this assurance. The conditions which justified him in this course of thought and method of writing must not be overlooked, if we are at all correctly to understand the conditions under which he wrote and the meaning of what he said, especially his meager statements concerning the authorship of New Testament writings.

If we thus put the testimony of the letters and the testimony from the presbyters together, reading both in view of the apologetic purpose with which Irenaeus wrote, recognizing that he was concerned with authorship only in a most incidental way, we come to see that the testimony which Irenaeus gives us is all the more important because it is incidental and that it is worth much more than its meager expression appears at first to indicate. We are able, in fact, partially to restore the conditions of Irenaeus' time and to understand why his language is what we find.

At the same time, however, although this partial restoration has given us the son of Zebedee as the John of Asia together with actual Johannine writings, our fourth gospel in its present form has removed from the close of the first century to the middle of the second. This conclusion, at once extremely conservative and highly radical, has been reached, however, only by a most thorough and painstaking investigation of the data bearing on the problem.

As compared with the investigation of Lightfoot, the essay has frankly opened the question of the "authenticity" of the gospel without regard to results, and the outcome has been a truly Johannine foundation for the gospel which Lightfoot did not reach. In fact, he was hardly aware, perhaps, of the seriousness of the task of showing a closeness of relationship between the gospel and the son of Zebedee; his personal religious attitude and his ecclesiastical position made indubitable for him arguments which, to another cast of mind, possess little convincing power. The discussion of this essay, without religious or ecclesiastical concern as to who wrote the gospel, has made it easier to estimate both Lightfoot's discussion and the cogency of such replies as that of Harnack and, with the aid of both, to go deeper into the problem than either.

As over against Harnack's study and conclusion specifically, I have shown; (1) that Irenaeus was in a position to know the facts, substantially at least, concerning the Asian John; (2) that, therefore, Irenaeus' testimony concerning John and the Johannine writings cannot be lightly set aside, and (3) that, when all the testimony bearing on the form of the presbyter material is taken into account, Irenaeus' source for this testimony is all seen to be oral tradition, rather than partially the writings of Papias, and, thereby, to reveal the near relation in which Irenaeus stood to the conditions of the first century. Out of this more careful study of those relations emerges the son of Zebedee as the only probable author of Johannine writings from which the fourth gospel was later compiled.

In somewhat similar manner, the confident, but unconvincing, argument of Zahn has been supplemented and his finding for the oral character of the presbyter testimony has been put on a stable foundation. This has been done by recognizing that his treatment, like that of Lightfoot, is insufficient, and by taking into account the very important item of presbyter testimony in the letter to Florinus.

Incidentally, the sweeping conclusion of de Boor and particularly that of Bacon and those who agree with these writers, that the son of Zebedee was an early martyr, has been found to be unwarranted in view of the best evidence bearing on the question. The symbolic language of the New Testament and the "silence" of Ignatius and others of his time have been sufficiently, or even better, explained on the theory that John lived to old age in Asia Minor.

The conclusions which have been reached may be summarized for convenience and somewhat more in detail as follows:

1. Irenaeus' quotations from the fourth gospel, or references to it, are sufficient to furnish a probability that he had the gospel in substantially the same form in which we have it (pp. 10–16).

2. His use of the language of the gospel, generally, was quite free, and his manner of attributing it to different persons or sources was interestingly diversified (pp. 11–13). These phenomena, together with the fact that he sometimes placed a higher estimate on oral gospel testimony than on the written gospel (pp. 54–56), and his sparing use of the gospel outside of the prologue (p. 12), indicate how highly he regarded the oral accounts of Jesus' life and teachings which had come down to him.

3. The testimony which Irenaeus referred to the presbyters is oral throughout (p. 50) and corroborates the closeness of Irenaeus' relation to the apostles, which he sometimes asserted but oftener assumed (p. 57). One of these presbyters was Polycarp (p. 48). One of the unnamed presbyters was of the second generation from the apostles (p. 47) and yet had evidently lived earlier than Irenaeus. Other men, in similar ways, must have overlapped the period between the chief activities of Polycarp and the beginning of the manhood of Irenaeus in such a way as to give body to the traditions which have come down to us chiefly in the name of Polycarp (pp. 51–53). Such men were in an excellent position to know the state of affairs and the opinions during the first half of the second century and to be the means of the transmission of these to the days of Irenaeus.

4. The testimony of Irenaeus, therefore, though not a critical estimate of the testimony of his predecessors, and though coming from the last quarter of the second century, is substantially the testimony of Polycarp and men associated with him, testimony which these men were accustomed to give during the first half of the second century, or even, in the case of Polycarp's younger contemporaries, over into the second half of the century (pp. 24 f.).

5. Polycarp was a man some thirty years of age at the close of the first century (p. 26). He had associated with other apostolic men as well as John (p. 28). Accordingly, he was in a position to know accurately of Christian affairs at the close of the first century, of the men who were then in Asia, of the accounts of their lives then current, and of their teachings. Out of such a situation developed the Polycarp-Irenaeus testimony concerning John and the Johannine gospel. This testimony knows only one John of apostolic times other than John the Baptist and John Mark (pp. 17, 30). This one John, though he is not specifically called the son of Zebedee, was certainly the man whom we call the son of Zebedee.

6. Irenaeus, Florinus, Polycarp, and those of their time, i. e., back to the beginning of the second century, appear to have been familiar with

written Johanno-Asian accounts of the life and teachings of Jesus, with which Polycarp's oral accounts used to be compared (pp. 31-38), and the people of those days knew no other author of these than the son of Zebedee (p. 39). This was the only view current until after Irenaeus' time, and this unanimity of opinion concerning the authorship of the Johannine gospel helps to explain why so little is extant in the literature of the second century concerning the authorship (p. 39).

7. While we are warranted, on the basis of the Irenaeus testimony, in saying that Irenaeus had the fourth gospel in substantially the same form in which it has come to us, we are not warranted by that testimony in saying that the gospel was in existence in its present form at the close of the first century. As far as Irenaeus' testimony can assure us, the Johanno-Asian accounts of the life and teachings of Jesus at the time of Polycarp were in the form of separate and brief narratives, or booklets (pp. 35-37).

APPENDIX
RESULTING HYPOTHESIS FOR THE JOHANNINE QUESTIONS

Lest this conclusion should leave indefinite the meaning which it gives for the Johannine questions as a whole, I venture to suggest the general Johannine hypothesis to which it leads. Its most important elements are the following:

1. John did not write a single and complete account of the life and teachings of Jesus. Perhaps he was never inclined to do so. He did, however, in connection with his ministry in Asia, either write short accounts, or, perhaps still more probably, allow some one of his disciples to write such accounts of what he used to say to the people. These accounts were frequently short sermons founded on the life and work of Jesus. As such, they were not intended to be mere history but rather interpretations of Jesus, sometimes in allegorical form, for the people to whom John spoke.

2. Those written sermons, or booklets, were treasured up even before the death of John, but, naturally, they came to be prized more highly after his death. The apparent references to the fourth gospel in the literature up to the time of Justin may reflect the existence of these booklets and indicate the place which they possessed for the Christians who knew them, who were probably a considerable portion of the Christians of Asia, at least. In this form they were not thought of as a gospel.

3. Somewhere about the middle of the second century, some one—Polycarp is perhaps as naturally thought of as anyone—conceived the idea of combining such of these sermons as were suitable to the purpose into a gospel which would present aspects of the life and teaching of Jesus supplementary to the aspects of his life and teaching portrayed in the gospels already in circulation. This editorial work was performed and the book duly published.

4. This gospel, thus produced out of material which was already recognized as John's and needing no explanation of its origin, was at once accepted and soon took its place with those which had received their current form much earlier. If we had all the correspondence of the time and notes of all the oral news which then passed among the Christians, we should probably find some reference to such a course of events for the Johannine writings. As conditions were, such material was too unimportant and too little thought of to warrant its preservation. This acceptance and use of

the Johannine gospel naturally occurred first in Asia. In view of Irenaeus' close relationship with Asia, a copy went to him promptly, and he accepted it without hesitation as the connected form of the gospel which he had heard from Polycarp and the collection of the Johannine writings which he had known in his youth. If the gospel was published about the time of the death of Polycarp, at his suggestion, and, on the part of those who carried out his wish, as a memorial treasury, perhaps, of the Johannine tradition which no one else so directly preserved, it would have reached Irenaeus while he was still a young man. In that case, he would have felt the least possible cause for giving any special attention to the detailed events through which the gospel arose or for hesitating to use it as John's gospel. Throughout the Christian world it was soon recognized as the written form of the story of Jesus which was already so well known through the oral tradition of the presbyters and, in Asia at least, through the booklets out of which it had been compiled.

5. Some of the Johannine sermons were on other subjects than the life of Jesus. The first Johannine letter is to be explained from such fragments. The second and third may have arisen in this way, but perhaps the probability is against this theory. They are more likely to be actual letters from John.

6. The Apocalypse, like all other apocalypses, is a pseudonymous work. Its author availed himself of the fame of John in Asia and perhaps made use of some of the Johannine material. He published his work in Rome, or at least in the West, about the middle of the second century, perhaps under cover of the appearance of the gospel. Under these conditions, together with the hospitable apocalyptic atmosphere of the time, its ready acceptance in the West but much slower acceptance in the East was a natural phenomenon. By the time Justin wrote his *Dialogue* it had gained sufficient recognition in the West to be referred to as corroborative testimony (chap. 81). Irenaeus, like others of his time in the West, accepted the book without hesitation.

INDEX OF NAMES AND SUBJECTS

Abbreviations, 9, 10
Alogi, 39
Anicetus, 25
Apocalypse, the, 31, 62
Apostle, Irenaeus' use, 20–22
Apostolic times, extent, 17
Asia, communication with the west, 25, 53

Bacon, B. W., 30, 41, 50

Cerinthus, 39, 40
Clement of Alexandria, 13
Conybeare, F. C., 55

De Boor, 30
"Disciple," the, 20
Documents and tradition, 52
Drummond, James, 42

ἐγγράφως, 50
Epiphanius, 39
Eusebius, 24, 31

Florinus, letter to, 26–29
Fourth gospel—
  Work of John of Asia, 17
  In time of Polycarp, 33–38
  Origin for Irenaeus, 37
  Compared with presbyter testimony, 54
  Date of compilation, 36, 61

γραφαῖς, ταῖς, 31–39

Harnack, A., 27, 42, 43, 47, 50
Heresies, The, a tract for the times, 51

Ignatius, 31, 53
Irenaeus, use of gospel, 12
—Looseness of style, 39
—Theological development, 15
—Terminology that of New Testament, 20

—Relation to Polycarp's testimony, 26, 40
—Communication with Asia, 25, 29, 51, 53
—How to be understood, 52

Jackson, H. L., 19
Jameses, did Irenaeus confuse? 22
Jesus' age, 45, 54
John of Asia, apostle, 18, 23, 29, 30
—And Johannine writings, 31, 39, 58
John, gospel of. *See* Fourth gospel
Johannine letters, 62
John Mark, 17
John the Baptist, 17, 20
Justin Martyr, 34, 62

Lightfoot, J. B., 42, 43
Luke, gospel of, 24

Monnier, 21

Oncken, Johann, 52

Papias, 31, 32, 49
Polycarp, 25, 27, 28, 31, 34, 48
Presbyter testimony, the, 41–51
—Superior to gospels, 54
—Compared with letters to Victor and Florinus, 55
Presbyters' names, why not given, 53
Prologue, use by Irenaeus, 12

Scott, C. A., 19
Scott, E. F., 5
Swete, H. B., 19

Trajan, 17, 18

Victor, letter to, 24

Zahn, T., 41 ff., 50

INDEX OF PASSAGES IN IRENAEUS

	PAGE		PAGE		PAGE
1. p. 2a	42	3. 11. 8	54	4. 8. 3b	22
1. 3. 5b	17	3. 11. 9c	21	4. 20. 11b	13
1. 13. 3c	42	3. 12. 3a	21	4. 25. 3b	9
1. 15. 6	42	3. 12. 5a	19	4. 26. 2a	21
1. 30. 12b	17	3. 12. 8a	21	4. 27–32	42, 44, 47, 50
2. 9. 1c	21	3. 12. 10a	21	4. 33. 8a	21
2. 22	20	3. 12. 15c	21, 22	4. 41. 2a	42, 50
2. 22. 3	15	3. 14. 1a	17	5. 5. 1c	42, 44, 47
2. 22. 5c 17, 42 ff., 53, 56		3. 16. 1	19	5. 17. 4b	17
		3. 17. 4c	42	5. 17. 4c	42
3. 1. 1c 13, 21, 24, 37, 55		3. 19. 3c	55	5. 20. 1	21
3. 3. 3c	21	3. 21. 3c	19	5. 28. 4c	53
3. 3. 4	17, 18, 28, 53	3. 21. 4a	21	5. 30. 1a	42, 44, 47
3. 5. 1a	18, 21	3. 23. 3a	42	5. 33. 3b	42, 44, 46
3. 10. 3	13, 17			5. 33. 4	49, 53
3. 11. 1	39, 40	4. p. 2b	42	5. 36. 1	42, 44
3. 11. 4c	20	4. 4. 2b	42	5. 36. 2a	54
3. 11. 4–9	42	4. 4. 3b	17		

INDEX OF NEW TESTAMENT TEXTS

Matt. 1:18	21	John 8:56, 57	54	John 19:26, 27	20
28:19	55	chap. 10	13	20:2, 3, 4, 8	20
Luke 1:35	21	13:25	13	chap. 21	13
John 1:18	13	14:2	54	21:7, 20, 23, 24	20
3:18–21	13	14:6	19		
8:44	13	18:15, 16	20		

www.ingramcontent.com/pod-product-compliance
Lightning Source LLC
Chambersburg PA
CBHW061512040426
42450CB00008B/1585